THE
BIG BOOK
OF AIR FRYER
RECIPES

THE
BIG BOOK
OF AIR FRYER
RECIPES

240 Standout Recipes with
240 Gorgeous Photos for Healthy,
Delicious Meals

PARRISH RITCHIE

Founder of
Life With The Crust
Cut Off

PAGE STREET
PUBLISHING CO.

PAGE STREET
PUBLISHING CO.

First published in 2020 by

Page Street Publishing Co.

27 Congress Street, Suite 1511

Salem, MA 01970

www.pagestreetpublishing.com

Distributed by Macmillan, sales in Canada by The Canadian Manda Group.

25 24 23 22   5 6 7

ISBN-13: 978-1-64567-100-8

ISBN-10: 1-64567-100-3

Library of Congress Control Number: 2019957243

Cover and book design by Kylie Alexander for Page Street Publishing Co.

Photography by Parrish Ritchie

Printed and bound in China

DEDICATION

TO MY HUSBAND, DANIEL,
FOR ALWAYS HOLDING MY HAND
THROUGH EVERYTHING.

TO MY BROTHER CHRISTOPHER, ONE OF MY
BIGGEST SUPPORTERS. I WILL MISS YOU
FOREVER. 1988–2020

TABLE OF CONTENTS

INTRODUCTION

Hey! I'm Parrish, a food blogger, cookbook author, wife to the milkman—yes, milkmen still exist and deliver milk to your door!—and mom of two crazy little boys. Being a busy mom, I know how hard it can be to get a meal on the table, especially a meal everyone will eat (I strive for at least three out of four). So I love to share family-friendly, crowd-pleasing recipes anyone can make and everyone will love.

Air fryers are all the rage right now, and for good reason. These machines are amazing. They have changed the way I cook. I use my air fryer almost every day, multiple times a day.

So what does an air fryer do? It is basically a mini convection oven but better! An air fryer will cook your food in half the time an oven will, saving you so much time in the kitchen. It also fries food without the need for cups of oil. Most of these recipes deliver deep-fried crunch with only teaspoons of oil—in some cases, a few spritzes of spray oil is all you need to get crispy, crunchy food right from the air fryer.

When I first got my air fryer, I was amazed at how it cooked frozen nuggets to perfection, crisped those leftover take-out fries back to deliciousness and made really good pork chops. But those foods were all I was using it for.

Then I started experimenting. Oh my goodness, almost everything you put in the air fryer comes out better than if you cooked it on the stove or in the oven. This past summer, I didn't turn my oven on once—I cooked everything in my air fryer without heating up my kitchen at all!

In this book, I will show you how to make amazing dishes in your air fryer that you would have never thought of: things like Bulgogi Beef Jerky (page 63), Air Fryer Rainbow Bagels (page 102), Ham and Pineapple Fried Rice (page 283) and even dessert.

These recipes are my family's favorites. I am a busy mama and the air fryer saves me time, so I compiled this book of easy, fast, crowd-pleasing recipes because making your life easier is the point of the air fryer! All the easy-to-follow recipes in this book use simple ingredients you can get right at your store, making even your grocery shopping a little easier. You will be surprised at how many delicious and amazing meals you can make in no time using your air fryer.

P. Parrish ♡

A LITTLE INFORMATION ABOUT YOUR AIR FRYER
(AND SOME TIPS AND HINTS)

You probably already love your air fryer and have made a few things in it. But there are some things to talk about to make air-frying easier.

There are a million different air fryers out there; they come in all shapes and sizes. The air fryer you have may not be the air fryer I use. I used a 5.8-quart (5.6-L), basket-style Cosori Air Fryer for all the recipes in this book. Your air fryer may be a different size; therefore, you might have to do things in one or two more batches than you would using a larger air fryer (or if yours is bigger, you might need to cook things in only one batch).

Air fryers vary with the cooking times across all the different brands. Get a feel for your air fryer—yours might cook a little faster, a little hotter or a little slower. Once you know how your air fryer cooks, you can see if you need to add a minute or two to the listed cook time or maybe take things out a little earlier. When I'm making a new recipe in my air fryer, I keep an eye on it, check it and adjust the times as needed.

You will see I often use parchment rounds in my recipes; they make cleanup easier and help keep food from sticking. You can cut parchment rounds to fit your air fryer, but you can buy big packs of them for next to nothing on Amazon.

Invest in a good accessory kit. Everything I use in my air fryer came as one bundle from Amazon. It is important to find a deep baking dish and cake pans that fit your air fryer. My bundle also came with the egg molds for my air fryer, which I use to make my Spicy Spinach Egg Bites (page 117) and Bacon–Pepper Jack Egg Bites (page 126). Some of the recipes call for a 1- to 2-quart (960-ml to 1.9-L) baking dish, and I list it as such so you can get one that fits your air fryer. The baking dish I used for these recipes is 1½ quarts (1.4 L). I also have some good ramekins that fit perfectly in my air fryer.

A meat thermometer is a good idea. I like to make sure my meat is cooked properly by using a meat thermometer. These are relatively inexpensive and are a great way to make sure everything is cooked to the proper temperature.

I use my air fryer for everything, and I hope you will love your air fryer and these recipes as much as I do.

STARTERS AND SMALL BITES

I love to entertain, host parties, throw holiday get-togethers and have our friends over for cards. All of these require appetizers or snacks, and I am that lady who is rushing around at the last minute (or even after guests have arrived) to switch out whatever is in the oven for the next dish. My kitchen gets hot, my guests get hot and it's just a hot mess!

My entertaining style changed when I got my air fryer. It makes hosting so much easier. I can throw what I need in the air fryer, and not only does it come out tastier, crispier and crunchier than it would from the oven but I'm also not adding any heat to my house.

Because the air fryer cooks things quickly, I am able to make more of a certain kind of appetizer and I am able to make a greater variety. We love making egg rolls and fried pickles for get-togethers, but who wants to stand in front of a big pan of stinky oil all throughout the party? Not me!

With my air fryer, I can create many delicious appetizers for my social events, and I can even whip up quick snacks for a family movie night or an evening of cards with friends.

MAC AND CHEESE EGG ROLLS

Is there anything better than macaroni and cheese? Yes. Mac and Cheese Egg Rolls! Roll some macaroni and cheese up in an eggroll wrapper, let it get nice and crispy in the air fryer and you have an amazing snack everyone will love. You can even make these smaller and serve them as appetizers at parties.

In a large bowl, mix together the macaroni and cheese, Cheddar cheese and mozzarella cheese.

Spoon 1 to 2 tablespoons (13 to 26 g) of the macaroni and cheese mixture into each egg roll wrapper and tuck in the ends of the egg roll wrapper.

Moisten the edge of the egg roll wrapper with a bit of water and roll the egg roll up.

Spray the air fryer basket with the spray oil and place 2 egg rolls in the basket, seam side down. (Avoid placing them too close together.)

Spray the tops of the egg rolls with the spray oil and sprinkle them with the kosher salt. Air-fry the eggs rolls at 390°F (199°C) for 6 to 8 minutes, flipping them once.

Repeat this process with the remaining egg rolls.

Serve the egg rolls with the Buffalo sauce, barbecue sauce or ranch dressing.

TIP: You can add bacon or chicken to these to take them from fantastic to out of this world!

MAKES: 16 SERVINGS

3 cups (567 g) prepared macaroni and cheese

1 cup (120 g) shredded Cheddar cheese

½ cup (56 g) shredded mozzarella cheese

16 egg roll wrappers

Spray oil

Kosher salt

Buffalo sauce, barbecue sauce or ranch dressing, to serve

CAJUN AIR-FRIED PICKLES

Fried pickles are a family favorite around here. I swear we base our restaurant choices by whether they serve them. I was thrilled when I learned I could air-fry them! They take no time to make, I always have the ingredients on hand and I always have one happy family ready to dig in. I decided to add a little Cajun spice to these—it works perfectly!

Drain the pickle slices on a paper towel. Meanwhile, prepare three medium bowls for the coating. Place the flour in the first bowl. In the second bowl, beat together the eggs and hot sauce. In the third bowl, combine the panko bread crumbs, cornmeal and Cajun seasoning.

Spray the basket of the air fryer with the spray oil.

Dip each pickle slice in the flour, then in the egg mixture and finally in the panko-cornmeal mixture.

Place as many pickles as can fit in a single layer in the air fryer basket and spray them generously with the spray oil.

Air-fry the pickles at 400°F (204°C) for 7 minutes, then flip the pickles, spritz them with spray oil and air-fry for 5 minutes.

Repeat this process with the remaining pickles.

Serve the pickles with the ranch dressing.

MAKES:
4 SERVINGS

32 pickle slices of choice

½ cup (60 g) all-purpose flour

3 large eggs

2 tsp (10 ml) hot sauce

1 cup (55 g) panko bread crumbs

1 cup (170 g) cornmeal

1 tbsp (9 g) Cajun seasoning

Spray oil

Ranch dressing, to serve

CRISPY SPINACH MOZZARELLA STICKS

My husband and I used to frequent this cute little diner that served the best mozzarella sticks. The mozzarella sticks had spinach in them and were wrapped in crispy egg roll wrappers. When I got my air fryer, I knew these would be perfect to replicate at home. The air fryer makes the egg roll wrappers super crispy without actually frying them, the cheese inside gets all melty and delicious and the garlicky spinach puts a new spin on this classic appetizer. Since these cook up in minutes, you can make them anytime!

In a small skillet over medium heat, melt the butter. Add the spinach and garlic and sauté until the spinach has cooked down, 5 to 8 minutes. Set the spinach aside to cool.

Meanwhile, cut each string cheese stick in half for a total of 12 short sticks.

Cut each egg roll wrapper in half for a total of 12 wrappers. Place ½ teaspoon of the spinach mixture on the short edge of the egg roll wrapper and spread it out thinly (but not all the way to the edges).

Place a cheese stick half on the egg roll wrapper next to the spinach. Fold in the sides of the wrapper and then roll up the egg roll lengthwise.

Spritz the air fryer basket with the spray oil and place the egg rolls in the basket, seam side down.

Spray the egg rolls with additional spray oil and sprinkle them with the salt.

Air-fry the mozzarella sticks at 375°F (191°C) for 7 to 8 minutes, flipping the mozzarella sticks once halfway through the cooking time. They should be brown and crispy.

Serve the mozzarella sticks with warmed marinara sauce and Parmesan cheese for dipping.

MAKES: 12 EGG ROLLS

½ tbsp (8 g) butter or ½ tbsp (8 ml) oil of choice

2 cups (60 g) baby spinach, finely chopped

1 clove garlic, minced

6 sticks mozzarella string cheese

6 egg roll wrappers

Spray oil

Salt

Marinara sauce, warmed, to serve

Parmesan cheese, to serve

TIP: These can be made in advance and frozen.

PIZZA SOFT PRETZELS

Soft pretzels are my boys' favorite part of going to the mall. They especially like the pizza-topped ones. (And let's be honest—so do I!) Now I can make their favorite soft pretzels right at home in just minutes. These are great for an after-school snack or movie-night treat.

Slice the pizza dough into 8 strips.

Twist each strip into a pretzel by making a U shape and then twisting the ends together and securing them to the bottom of the U shape.

In a small bowl, mix together the butter and garlic salt. Brush this mixture onto each pretzel. Top each pretzel with the mozzarella cheese and pepperoni. Sprinkle the desired amount of Parmesan cheese over the top of each pretzel.

Place 4 pretzels (or however many will fit without touching) in the air fryer and air-fry the pretzels at 350°F (177°C) for 5 minutes.

Repeat this process with the remaining pretzels.

Serve the pretzels with the marinara sauce or ranch dressing for dipping.

TIP: Throw on your other favorite pizza toppings and make these all your own!

MAKES:
8 PRETZELS

1 (14-oz [397-g]) can pizza dough

3 tbsp (45 ml) melted butter

1 tsp garlic salt

¾ to 1 cup (84 to 112 g) shredded mozzarella cheese

¼ cup (35 g) mini pepperoni slices

Grated Parmesan cheese

Marinara sauce or ranch dressing, to serve

PARMESAN-RANCH CRISPY CHICKPEAS

Did you know that you can make chickpeas into a delicious, crispy, poppable snack? Did you also know that you could do it in your air fryer in mere minutes? Well, you can, and they are amazing! These have a great flavor, and they get addictively crunchy and are a perfect snack for any time of day. Whip up a few batches of these in the beginning of the week and you will have a great snack all week long.

In a medium bowl, mix together the Parmesan cheese, ranch dressing mix, black pepper, garlic salt and oil. Gently toss the chickpeas in the seasoning mixture to coat them.

Put all the chickpeas into the air fryer and air-fry them at 390°F (199°C) for 12 to 15 minutes, shaking a few times during the cooking process.

Let the chickpeas cool before serving.

TIP: You can season these any way you like; for example, add some cayenne pepper for a kick!

MAKES:
2 TO 3 SERVINGS

1 tsp grated Parmesan cheese

½ tsp ranch dressing mix

¼ tsp black pepper

¼ tsp garlic salt

½ tbsp (8 ml) oil of choice

1 (15.5-oz [439-g]) can chickpeas, drained and rinsed

SOUTHWEST AVOCADO EGG ROLLS WITH SPICY RANCH DIPPING SAUCE

These egg rolls are my favorite appetizer ever. I get them at any restaurant that serves them and I make them frequently at home. Of course, they were one of the first things I tried in my air fryer—and I was not disappointed! I serve these with an easy spicy ranch that has a bit of a kick.

MAKES: APPROXIMATELY 20 EGG ROLLS

1 tbsp (15 g) butter or 1 tbsp (15 ml) oil of choice

1 small onion, diced

1 small bell pepper (any color), diced

1 clove garlic, minced

½ cup (72 g) canned or frozen corn

½ cup (30 g) black beans, drained and rinsed

1 (4-oz [112-g]) can diced green chilis, drained

1 cup (112 g) shredded pepper Jack cheese

1 cup (120 g) shredded Cheddar cheese

2 medium avocados, diced

20 egg roll wrappers

Spray oil

Kosher salt

1 cup (240 ml) ranch dressing

1 tbsp (15 ml) adobo sauce from chipotles in adobo

In a small skillet over medium heat, combine the butter, onion and bell pepper and cook until the onion is translucent, about 10 minutes. Add the garlic and cook for 1 minute before turning off the heat.

Transfer the vegetables to a large bowl. Add the corn, black beans, green chilis, pepper Jack cheese and Cheddar cheese. Mix to combine. Carefully stir in the avocado chunks.

Place about 2 tablespoons (30 g) of the filling into each egg roll wrapper. Fold over the ends of the wrapper and roll up the wrapper, moistening the edge with water to seal the egg roll.

Repeat this process until all the egg roll wrappers are filled.

Spray the air fryer basket with the spray oil. Place the egg rolls, seam side down, in the air fryer basket. Spray the egg rolls with the spray oil and sprinkle a little of the kosher salt on each one.

Air-fry the egg rolls at 375°F (191°C) for 7 to 10 minutes, flipping once halfway through the cooking time.

In a small bowl, combine the ranch dressing with the adobo sauce and stir well.

Serve the egg rolls with the spicy ranch dipping sauce.

STUFFED CREAM CHEESE BITES

These are one of my favorite snacks. The warm, gooey cream cheese makes these bites irresistible. You can create these perfect little bites in just minutes, and they make a quick snack that's a bit different.

Cut the pizza dough into 12 squares.

In a medium bowl, combine the cream cheese and powdered sugar until they are well mixed.

Divide the filling among the 12 pieces of dough. Wrap the dough around the filling and roll it into a ball, making sure there are no open seams.

Spray the air fryer basket lightly with the spray oil. Place four or five bites in the air fryer basket at a time. Brush the tops of the bites with the butter and sprinkle them with sesame seeds (if using).

Air-fry the bites at 350°F (177°C) for 5 minutes. Repeat this process with the remaining bites.

Serve the bites warm.

**MAKES:
12 BITES**

1 (14-oz [397-g]) can pizza dough

8 oz (227 g) cream cheese, softened

½ cup (65 g) powdered sugar

Spray oil

2 tbsp (30 g) butter, melted

Sesame seeds (optional)

TIP: Skip the sesame seeds and top the bites with a sprinkle of cinnamon sugar for a sweeter treat.

PHILLY CHEESESTEAK EGG ROLLS

We have the best sub shop around here that opened the year I was born, and we still go there a few times a month! They just recently added cheesesteak egg rolls to their menu, and I knew I could use my trusty air fryer to whip up my own version of this delicious snack. I use pepper Jack cheese because my mom and I love adding hot peppers to our cheesesteaks for a little kick.

In a medium skillet over medium-high heat, melt the butter. Add the onion and bell pepper and cook them for 10 minutes, until the onion is translucent. Add the ground beef, salt and black pepper.

Cook the mixture for 8 to 10 minutes, until the meat is cooked through. Set the mixture aside to cool slightly before handling.

Lay out an egg roll wrapper and add a bit of the provolone cheese and some of the pepper Jack cheese. Add 2 to 3 tablespoons (30 to 45 g) of the meat mixture.

Fold both the short ends of the egg roll wrapper inward, and then roll up the egg roll lengthwise. Moisten the edge with a little water to seal the egg roll.

Place 4 to 6 egg rolls in the air fryer, seam side down, and spray them with the spray oil. Sprinkle the egg rolls with the kosher salt.

Air-fry the egg rolls at 375°F (191°C) for 8 minutes, flipping once halfway through the cooking time. Repeat this process with the remaining egg rolls.

MAKES: 15 TO 20 EGG ROLLS

1 tbsp (15 g) butter

1 small sweet onion, diced

1 small green bell pepper, diced

1 lb (450 g) ground beef

½ tsp salt

½ tsp black pepper

15 to 20 egg roll wrappers

5 slices provolone cheese, coarsely chopped

1½ cups (168 g) shredded pepper Jack cheese

Spray oil

Kosher salt

TIP: You can use any cheese you like. American is a great choice. I like the white American cheese sold at the deli, as it melts beautifully.

SPINACH-RICOTTA TOASTED RAVIOLI

Toasted ravioli is on every appetizer menu because it is so delicious. It also is a cinch to make, especially in the air fryer! These toasted ravioli come out crispy and cheesy. What more could you want in an appetizer? Be prepared to double the recipe—these are always the first to go.

Fill a large pot with water and bring it to a boil over high heat. Boil the ravioli for 2 to 3 minutes. Drain the ravioli and set them aside.

Place the eggs in a shallow bowl. In another shallow bowl, mix together the traditional bread crumbs, panko bread crumbs, garlic salt, Italian seasoning and Parmesan cheese.

Dip each ravioli in the eggs and then dip it into the bread crumb mixture.

Spray the bottom of the air fryer with the spray oil, and then place a single layer of the ravioli in the basket. Spray the tops of the ravioli with the spray oil.

Air-fry the ravioli at 400°F (204°C) for 8 minutes, flipping once during the cooking time.

Repeat this process with the remaining ravioli.

Serve the ravioli warm with marinara sauce.

**MAKES:
4 TO 6 SERVINGS**

1 (18-oz [510-g]) package frozen or refrigerated spinach-cheese ravioli

3 large eggs, beaten

1 cup (120 g) traditional bread crumbs

1 cup (55 g) panko bread crumbs

2 tsp (6 g) garlic salt

1 tsp Italian seasoning

1 cup (180 g) grated Parmesan cheese

Spray oil

Marinara sauce, to serve

TIP: You can make this with your favorite flavor of ravioli. Switch it up and try Alfredo sauce for dipping.

BLACK BEAN AND CORN MINI PEPPERS

Looking for a lighter appetizer that is still full of flavor? These stuffed mini peppers are the answer! Full of corn and black beans, these little snacks get great flavor from pepper Jack cheese. These take just minutes to prep and minutes to cook in the air fryer, making them the perfect snack. We love making them for a night of TV bingeing.

In a large bowl, mix together the garlic salt, cream cheese and pepper Jack cheese until they are well blended. Gently stir in the black beans and corn. Stuff each pepper with the black bean and corn mixture.

Place the stuffed peppers in the air fryer basket in a single layer. Air-fry them at 360°F (182°C) for 10 minutes.

Garnish the mini peppers with the sour cream and green onion (if using).

TIP: Switch the pepper Jack for Cheddar for a milder taste.

MAKES:
2 TO 3 SERVINGS

⅛ tsp garlic salt

¼ cup (60 g) cream cheese, softened

¼ cup (28 g) shredded pepper Jack cheese

¼ cup (15 g) black beans, drained and rinsed

¼ cup (36 g) canned corn

6 to 8 mini peppers, halved and seeded

Sour cream (optional)

Coarsely chopped green onion (optional)

RANCH SNACK MIX

This ranch snack mix is where it's at! It's simple to make and packed with flavor. I like to whip up a big batch of this and keep it on hand for snacks all week long. For parties, I put out a big bowl of this and everyone goes crazy. Thanks to the air fryer, this amazing snack is ready in minutes.

In a small bowl, combine the oil, ranch dressing mix and garlic salt. Stir until the ingredients are thoroughly mixed.

Place the oyster and Cheddar crackers and oil mixture in a 1-gallon (3.8-L) ziplock bag. Seal the bag and toss until the crackers are well coated in the oil mixture.

Place half of the snack mix in the air fryer. Air-fry at 300°F (149°C) for 7 minutes, shaking the basket once or twice. Repeat this process with the remaining half of the snack mix.

Let the snack mix cool before serving.

TIP: You can substitute mini pretzels for either kind of cracker if you like.

MAKES:
8 CUPS (435 G)

¼ cup (60 ml) vegetable oil

1 (1-oz [28-g]) packet ranch dressing mix

1 tsp garlic salt

1 (9-oz [255-g]) bag oyster crackers

1 (6.5-oz [184-g]) bag small Cheddar crackers

PEPPER JELLY— CREAM CHEESE PINWHEELS

One of my most popular recipes is a good old southern pepper jelly–cream cheese dip. We have it all the time at my house and the flavor combo is amazing. I knew the dip would be delicious rolled up in these flaky pinwheels. Yum!

In a small bowl, mix together the cream cheese and the pepper jelly until they are combined.

Press together two triangle crescents to make a rectangle. Repeat this step until you have four rectangles. Spread a quarter of the pepper jelly–cream cheese mixture on each rectangle.

Roll up each rectangle lengthwise. Slice it into 4 to 5 pinwheels.

Lightly spray the air fryer basket with the spray oil.

Place the pinwheels in the air fryer basket in a single layer. You may need to work in batches.

Air-fry the pinwheels at 320°F (160°C) for 6 to 8 minutes.

TIP: You can also use green jalapeño jelly if you can't find the red pepper jelly.

MAKES: 16 TO 20 PINWHEELS

4 oz (112 g) cream cheese, softened

3 tbsp (60 g) red pepper jelly

1 (8-oz [224-g]) can crescent rolls

Spray oil

CHEESY CORN TORTILLA CUPS

These Cheesy Corn Tortilla Cups are delicious! They take just minutes to prepare and minutes to cook in the air fryer. Creamy cheese with a little kick of heat melds perfectly with the sweetness of the corn and the salty crunch of the chips. Try these at your next party.

In a medium bowl, mix together the cream cheese, pepper Jack cheese, egg and corn until the ingredients are combined. Place about 1½ teaspoons (8 g) of the filling in each chip.

Place as many tortilla cups as you can fit in a single layer in the air fryer basket.

Air-fry the tortilla cups at 350°F (177°C) for 5 to 6 minutes. Repeat this process with the remaining tortilla cups.

Garnish the tortilla cups with the green onion (if using).

TIP: You can substitute Cheddar cheese for the pepper Jack.

MAKES:
12 SERVINGS

8 oz (227 g) cream cheese, softened

1 cup (112 g) shredded pepper Jack cheese

1 large egg

½ cup (72 g) drained corn

48 bowl- or scoop-shaped tortilla chips

Green onion, coarsely chopped (optional)

PINEAPPLE TERIYAKI SHRIMP

I don't think anything goes together better than pineapple, teriyaki and shrimp. We used to grill these shrimp—but once I got my air fryer I began making them in it, and now we can have these delicious little bites rain or shine. These are great for a party, but make sure to have plenty—they are a crowd favorite!

Drain the pineapple juice into a medium bowl and set the pineapple chunks aside. Add the teriyaki sauce to the bowl and mix well. Add the shrimp and toss to coat the shrimp in the sauce.

Skewer one shrimp and one chunk of pineapple on a toothpick. Repeat this process for the remaining shrimp and pineapple chunks.

Lay the skewers in the air fryer basket in a single layer. You will have to work in batches.

Air-fry the skewers at 400°F (204°C) for 3 to 5 minutes, until the shrimp are pink. (Check on them at 3 minutes and increase the cooking time if needed.)

TIP: You can skip the skewers and serve this recipe over rice for a delicious dinner.

MAKES:
30 SHRIMP

1 (20-oz [567-g]) can pineapple chunks in juice, undrained, divided

1 cup (240 ml) teriyaki sauce

30 large to extra-large raw shrimp, shells removed and deveined

FRIED DEVILED EGGS

Did you know you can hard-boil eggs in the air fryer? I figured it out and then had a ton of hard-boiled eggs, so I made these Fried Deviled Eggs. They are a delicious new twist on a classic. I like to just air-fry the whites and then add that glorious filling on top. These Fried Deviled Eggs are going to be a hit at all of your cookouts.

To make the eggs, hard-boil the eggs in the air fryer. Place the eggs in the air fryer and cook them at 270°F (132°C) for 15 minutes. After the 15 minutes have elapsed, immediately transfer the eggs to some cold water until they are cool enough to peel.

Slice the peeled eggs in half and scoop the yolks into a small bowl. To the egg yolks, add the mayonnaise, sugar, mustard, Worcestershire sauce, hot sauce and black pepper until the ingredients are smooth and combined. Stir in the bacon, reserving a tablespoon for topping.

To make the breading, mix together the flour, salt and black pepper in a shallow dish. In another shallow dish, beat the 2 eggs. Place the panko bread crumbs in a third shallow dish.

Take the egg white halves and dip them into the flour, shaking off the excess. Next, dip them in the beaten eggs. Finally, coat them in the panko bread crumbs.

Working in batches, place the egg whites in the air fryer and spray them with the spray oil. Air-fry the eggs at 350°F (177°C) for 5 minutes. Flip the egg halves, spray them again and cook them for 3 to 5 minutes.

Carefully remove the fried egg whites and place them right side up on plate or platter. Let them cool completely.

Pipe or spoon the egg yolk filling into each egg and sprinkle the top with a little paprika and crumbled bacon.

MAKES:
12 DEVILED EGGS

Eggs

6 large eggs

2 tbsp (28 g) mayonnaise

1 tsp sugar

1 tsp yellow mustard

1 tsp Worcestershire sauce

Dash of hot sauce

Pinch of black pepper

3 to 4 slices bacon, cooked and crumbled, divided

Paprika

Breading

1 cup (120 g) all-purpose flour

¼ tsp salt

⅛ tsp black pepper

2 large eggs

2 cups (110 g) panko bread crumbs

Spray oil

CRISPY ONION PETALS

WITH DIPPING SAUCE

The best part of eating at any steak house (besides the steak) is, of course, the crispy onion petals with that delicious dipping sauce. Now you can make them at home!

To make the onion petals, peel the onions and slice off the top and bottom of each one. Cut the onions into eighths and separate the "petals."

Place three shallow bowls in a row to form a breading station. Place the flour in the first bowl. Place the eggs in the second bowl. In the third bowl, mix together the bread crumbs, paprika, garlic salt, black pepper and Cajun seasoning.

Dip the onion petals into the flour, then the egg and then the bread crumb mixture.

Spray the air fryer basket with the spray oil and lay a single layer of the petals in the basket. You will need to work in batches. Spray the tops of the petals with the spray oil.

Air-fry the onion petals at 350°F (177°C) for 10 to 12 minutes.

Meanwhile, make the dipping sauce. In a medium bowl, combine the mayonnaise, ketchup, horseradish sauce, paprika, salt, oregano, black pepper and cayenne pepper. Keep the sauce in the refrigerator until you are ready to serve.

Serve the onion petals with the dipping sauce.

**MAKES:
4 SERVINGS**

Onion Petals

2 small yellow or sweet onions

1 cup (120 g) all-purpose flour

3 large eggs, beaten

1 cup (120 g) traditional bread crumbs

2 tsp (6 g) paprika

1 tsp garlic salt

½ tsp black pepper

½ tsp Cajun seasoning

Spray oil

Dipping Sauce

½ cup (110 g) mayonnaise

1 tbsp (17 g) ketchup

2 tbsp (30 g) horseradish sauce

½ tsp paprika

¼ tsp salt

⅛ tsp dried oregano

Pinch of black pepper

½ tsp cayenne pepper

ROASTED EDAMAME WITH EVERYTHING SEASONING

These everything-seasoned roasted edamame are easy to make and delicious, not to mention a real crowd-pleaser! The seasoning on these is fun step away from the usual soy sauce flavoring (though that is delicious as well). These roast up in minutes and make a great snack.

To make the everything bagel seasoning, combine the sesame seeds, poppy seeds, onion flakes, garlic and kosher salt in a medium bowl.

To make the edamame, toss the frozen edamame with the oil, 2 teaspoons (6 g) of everything bagel seasoning and garlic salt in a large bowl.

Place the edamame in the air fryer basket and air-fry at 390°F (199°C) for 10 minutes.

TIP: These also make a great side dish with dinner or lunch!

MAKES: 4 SERVINGS

Everything Bagel Seasoning
¼ cup (40 g) sesame seeds

¼ cup (34 g) poppy seeds

3 tbsp (15 g) dried onion flakes

3 tbsp (30 g) dried minced garlic

2 tbsp (36 g) kosher salt

Edamame
4½ cups (698 g) frozen edamame

1 tbsp (15 ml) oil

½ tsp garlic salt

CRANBERRY BRIE BITES

This appetizer is gorgeous and delicious. While these Cranberry Brie Bites look elegant and are a hit at any party, they could not be easier to make. They take just minutes to prep—and even less time in the air fryer.

Place a Brie cube into each tart shell.

In a small bowl, combine the cranberry sauce, brown sugar and orange zest. Top each tart shell with a little of the cranberry sauce mixture.

Place as many tarts as will fit in a single layer in the air fryer basket.

Air-fry the bites at 350°F (177°C) for 5 to 7 minutes, until the Brie is melted.

TIP: Sprinkle the bites with more orange zest or crushed pistachios for a festive look.

MAKES:
30 BITES

8 oz (227 g) Brie cheese, cut into 30 cubes

2 (1.9-oz [54-g]) boxes fully baked phyllo tart shells

1 (14-oz [397-g]) can whole cranberry sauce

2 tbsp (18 g) brown sugar

Zest of 1 small orange

JALAPEÑO POPPER PULL–APART BREAD

Who doesn't love warm, cheesy, flavorful bread? This Jalapeño Popper Pull-Apart Bread is my favorite to make. The flavors are amazing, and no one can get enough—you might want to double this recipe!

In a large bowl, mix together the butter, cream cheese and pepper Jack cheese.

Cut a crisscross pattern in the top of the bread, cutting into the loaf deeply but not all the way through.

Spread the butter-cheese mixture on the bread, making sure it gets in between the cuts.

Stick the jalapeños in between some of the cuts in the bread and lay a few on top.

Air-fry the bread at 400°F (204°C) for 5 minutes. Serve the bread warm with the ranch dressing for dipping (if using).

MAKES:
6 TO 8 SERVINGS

4 tbsp (60 g) butter, softened

6 oz (170 g) cream cheese, softened

2 cups (224 g) shredded pepper Jack cheese

1 round loaf bread

2 to 3 tbsp (18 to 27 g) jarred sliced jalapeños

Ranch dressing, to serve (optional)

LEMON-PEPPER WINGS

Oh, chicken wings, how I love to eat you and hate to make you. Or, I used to. My mom perfected crispy chicken wings in the oven, but they still took so long to cook. My son is obsessed with chicken wings with just a little garlic salt on them and requests them often. When I got my air fryer, I hoped it could make perfectly crispy chicken wings faster. I was not disappointed. These perfectly crisp chicken wings boast that great lemon-pepper flavor and a pop of garlic in less than half the time of traditional wings. Yum!

In a large bowl, toss the wings with the oil, garlic salt and lemon-pepper seasoning.

Place the wings in the air fryer basket in a single layer. You may have to work in batches.

Air-fry the wings at 400°F (204°C) for 18 to 20 minutes, flipping them once during the cooking time.

Serve these wings with the tzatziki sauce (if using).

MAKES:
3 TO 4 SERVINGS

1 lb (454 g) chicken wings

1 tbsp (15 ml) oil

1 tbsp (9 g) garlic salt

1 tbsp (9 g) lemon-pepper seasoning

Tzatziki sauce, to serve (optional)

SWEET AND SPICY CASHEWS

My whole family loves cashews, and I love them the most when they are extra toasty. I was having a get-together once and wanted to do a little something extra to the cashews. I spiced them with some honey and cayenne and let them get toasty in the air fryer. I got so many compliments on them. Be sure to whip these up the next time you have a party—they take only 10 minutes!

In a medium bowl, mix together the honey, sugar and cayenne pepper. Add the cashews and toss them in the honey mixture.

Place a parchment round in the bottom of the air fryer basket.

Place all the cashews in the air fryer and air-fry them at 350°F (177°C) for 8 minutes, shaking the basket once or twice during the cooking time.

While the cashews are cooking, line a large baking sheet with parchment paper. Transfer the cashews to the prepared baking sheet to cool before serving.

MAKES:
4 TO 6 SERVINGS

¼ cup (60 ml) honey

2 tbsp (24 g) sugar

1 tsp cayenne pepper

2 cups (220 g) salted cashews

SHRIMP TOAST

Shrimp toast is an amazingly easy appetizer that you don't see too often. This is traditionally deep-fried, but we are going to skip all that work and get these toasts crispy right in the air fryer.

In a food processor, combine the shrimp, cornstarch, egg, mayonnaise, salt and green onion. Pulse until a paste forms.

Spread the shrimp paste on one side of each piece of bread. Sprinkle the shrimp paste with the sesame seeds.

Spray the air fryer basket with the spray oil.

Place the pieces of bread in the air fryer basket in a single layer. You will have to work in batches. Spray the tops with a little spray oil.

Air-fry the bread at 350°F (177°C) for 5 minutes.

TIP: You can cut these into quarters for a smaller appetizer.

MAKES: 6 SERVINGS

8 oz (227 g) raw shrimp, peeled, deveined and tails removed

1 tbsp (9 g) cornstarch

1 large egg

1 tbsp (14 g) mayonnaise

½ tsp salt

2 tbsp (12 g) coarsely chopped green onion

6 slices white sandwich bread, halved diagonally

Sesame seeds

Spray oil

SALT AND VINEGAR PUMPKIN SEEDS

Fall is my favorite time of year. I love carving pumpkins and roasting pumpkin seeds. Did you know you can get the best crunchy pumpkin seeds using your air fryer? These pumpkin seeds are the best I've had—they are much crunchier than seeds roasted in the oven. I give them a quick soak in vinegar and toss them with salt for that tangy salt-and-vinegar flavor. So that you can enjoy this recipe year-round, I call for pumpkin seeds you can buy in the store. If you are using seeds from a fresh pumpkin, add 5 minutes to the cooking time.

In a medium bowl, mix together the pumpkin seeds and vinegar. Let the pumpkin seeds soak for about 5 minutes. Remove the seeds from the vinegar and place them in the air fryer basket.

Sprinkle the salt over the pumpkin seeds and toss them to coat them in the salt.

Air-fry the pumpkin seeds at 350°F (177°C) for 10 minutes, shaking the basket occasionally.

Let the pumpkin seeds cool before serving.

TIP: Try balsamic vinegar for a different flavor.

**MAKES:
1 CUP (120 G)**

1 cup (200 g) unsalted pumpkin seeds

¼ cup (60 ml) distilled white vinegar

1 tsp salt

BULGOGI BEEF JERKY

With my house full of boys, we can go through a lot of beef jerky—and my wallet is not happy about that. Then I found out that you can make beef jerky right in your air fryer. What a money saver! This jerky is our favorite, with sweet Asian flavors we can't get enough of! This recipe does require some patience, as it takes a while—with each air fryer being different, your jerky could take a little longer, so you might have to adjust the cook time accordingly.

In a large bowl, combine the soy sauce, vinegar, brown sugar, cola, garlic and green onions. Add the beef to the marinade and marinate the meat overnight in the refrigerator.

Remove the beef from the marinade and pat the meat dry.

Using metal skewers, pierce the top of the strips of meat and thread them through so they are hanging from the skewers.

Layer the skewers across the top of the air fryer basket so the beef strips hang down. Repeat this process with any remaining skewers.

Air-fry the beef at 180°F (82°C) for 1 hour. Let the jerky cool before serving.

TIP: If you do not have metal skewers, you can arrange the beef in a single layer in the basket of your air fryer, but you will have to work in batches and flip the meat halfway through the cooking time.

MAKES: 4 SERVINGS

¾ cup (180 ml) soy sauce

1 tbsp (15 ml) rice wine vinegar, distilled white vinegar or apple cider vinegar

1 cup (144 g) brown sugar

¾ cup (180 ml) cola

2 cloves garlic, minced

4 to 6 green onions, coarsely chopped

1 lb (450 g) bottom round beef, very thinly sliced

CREAM CHEESE WONTONS

Is there anyone who doesn't order cream cheese wontons with their Chinese takeout? They are the best part of the meal! Now you can make a big batch for yourself in less time than it takes to call for delivery. These cream cheese wontons get nice and crispy in the air fryer and are perfect for dipping into this easy sauce.

To make the wontons, mix together the cream cheese, green onion and Sriracha in a medium bowl until the mixture is smooth.

Place 2 teaspoons (10 g) of the cream cheese filling into each wonton wrapper.

Wet the edges of the wonton wrappers with a little water to seal the wontons. Pinch the corners of the wonton wrappers together so that they meet in the middle.

Spray the air fryer basket with the spray oil. Place a single layer of the wontons in the air fryer basket and spray them lightly with the spray oil.

Air-fry the wontons at 350°F (177°C) for 5 to 6 minutes, until they are crispy and golden brown.

To make the sauce, whisk together the cornstarch, vinegar, oil, pineapple juice, ketchup and brown sugar in a small pot over medium-low heat. Bring the sauce to a bubble while whisking and remove the sauce from the heat.

Serve the wontons with the sauce.

MAKES:
30 WONTONS

Wontons

8 oz (227 g) cream cheese, softened

2 tbsp (12 g) finely chopped green onion

1 tsp Sriracha, plus more if desired

30 wonton wrappers

Spray oil

Sauce

1 tsp cornstarch

1/3 cup (80 ml) distilled white vinegar

2 tsp (10 ml) vegetable oil

2/3 cup (160 ml) pineapple juice

2 tbsp (34 g) ketchup

3 tbsp (27 g) brown sugar

MOZZARELLA BRUSCHETTA

I use my air fryer to make toast for my bruschetta and roast some tomatoes for topping in this recipe, which means I can get double duty out of my air fryer. Bruschetta is a classic appetizer that is simple yet so full of flavor. The tomatoes become sweet and the bread crisp, all pairing beautifully with the creamy cheese, tangy balsamic and fresh bite of basil.

Place a parchment round in the air fryer basket.

In a small bowl, toss the cherry tomatoes with 1 tablespoon (15 ml) of the oil, garlic, salt and black pepper. Place the tomatoes in the air fryer basket and roast them at 400°F (204°C) for 8 to 10 minutes. Remove the tomatoes from the air fryer and set them aside.

Brush each side of the bread slices lightly with the remaining ½ cup (120 ml) of oil. Place as many slices as you can in a single layer in the air fryer basket. Toast the bread at 300°F (149°C) for 4 minutes.

Repeat this process until all of the bread is toasted.

Top each slice of toasted bread with a slice of the mozzarella cheese. Top each piece of toast with a few of the cherry tomatoes. Drizzle them all lightly with the balsamic vinegar.

Roll up the basil leaves and slice them thinly. Scatter them over the top of each piece of toast.

MAKES:
8 SERVINGS

1 cup (150 g) cherry tomatoes

1 tbsp (15 ml) plus ½ cup (120 ml) olive oil, divided

1 tsp minced garlic

½ tsp salt

¼ tsp black pepper

1 loaf of French bread, cut into 16 slices

1 lb (454 g) fresh mozzarella cheese, cut into 16 slices

Balsamic vinegar

Fresh basil leaves

POTATO AND PEA SAMOSAS

A delicious, flavorful filling of perfectly spiced potatoes and peas are nestled inside flaky little triangles. These spectacular samosas are ready and crispy in just minutes in the air fryer.

Heat the oil in a large skillet over medium heat. Add the onion, garlic, cumin, garam masala and turmeric and sauté the mixture for about 5 minutes, until the onion has just softened. Remove the skillet from the heat. Add the mashed potatoes, peas, cayenne pepper, salt and black pepper and stir to combine.

In a small bowl, whisk together the egg and water to create an egg wash. Set the bowl aside.

Cut the phyllo dough into equal squares and place about 1½ to 2 teaspoons (8 to 10 g) of the filling in the middle of each square. Fold the phyllo over into a triangle shape, using the egg wash to help seal the edges. Brush the tops of the samosas with the egg wash.

Spray the air fryer basket with the spray oil and place a single layer of samosas in the basket.

Spritz the tops of the samosas with spray oil.

Air-fry the samosas at 320°F (160°C) for 10 minutes, flipping once during the cooking time, until the samosas are crispy and brown. Repeat this process with the remaining samosas.

TIP: Serve these samosas with a mango chutney for a perfect pairing.

MAKES:
12 SERVINGS

1 tbsp (15 ml) olive oil

½ small onion, finely chopped

1 clove garlic, minced

1 tbsp (9 g) ground cumin

1 tsp garam masala

½ tsp ground turmeric

1½ lbs (680 g) russet potatoes, boiled and mashed

½ cup (75 g) frozen peas

½ tsp cayenne pepper

1 tsp salt

¼ tsp black pepper

1 large egg

1 tbsp (15 ml) water

5 sheets frozen phyllo dough, thawed

Spray oil

SOY-GLAZED SHISHITO PEPPERS

These roasted shishito peppers are so full of flavor and are perfect to serve when you are having a get-together—they are an unexpected addition to a charcuterie board! Don't let the fact that they are peppers scare you; they are very mild.

In a large bowl, toss together the shishito peppers, oil, soy sauce, honey, garlic and black pepper.

Place the shishito peppers in the air fryer basket. Air-fry the shishito peppers at 400°F (204°C) for 8 minutes, shaking the basket halfway through the cooking time.

**MAKES:
4 SERVINGS**

1 lb (454 g) shishito peppers

2 tbsp (30 ml) oil

1 tbsp (15 ml) soy sauce

1 tbsp (15 ml) honey

1 clove garlic, minced

¼ tsp black pepper

LOADED POTATO SKINS

Loaded potato skins are a classic appetizer and always a favorite. Who can resist crispy potato skins loaded with your favorite toppings and plenty of melty cheese? I use my air fryer to make baked potatoes, which I then turn into these delicious Loaded Potato Skins.

Wash and dry the potatoes. Rub each potato all over with the oil and sprinkle all sides with the salt. Transfer the potatoes to the air fryer basket.

Air-fry the potatoes at 380°F (193°C) for 30 minutes, flipping halfway through the cooking time. Check the potatoes to see if they are easily pierced with a fork; if not, air-fry them in 2-minute increments until they are cooked through.

Let the potatoes cool slightly, and then cut them in half. Scoop out some of the potatoes' flesh, leaving a shell (I like to leave a good amount of the potatoes' flesh in skins to make them more filling).

Sprinkle each potato skin with salt and black pepper, then sprinkle with the Cheddar cheese.

Divide the bacon among the potato skins. Return the potato skins to the air fryer and air-fry them at 350°F (177°C) for 3 to 5 minutes, until the cheese is melted.

Remove the potato skins from the air fryer and top each one with a dollop of sour cream and a few pieces of green onion.

MAKES:
6 SERVINGS

6 small baking potatoes

2 tbsp (30 ml) oil

Salt

Black pepper

½ to ¾ cup (60 to 90 g) shredded Cheddar cheese

12 slices bacon, cooked and crumbled

Sour cream

2 tbsp (12 g) coarsely chopped green onion

EGGPLANT FRIES WITH MARINARA

These eggplant fries are the perfect little appetizer for any get-together and make a great snack when you are craving something crispy and delicious. Serve them with some marinara for dipping—you will love them!

Place the flour in a shallow dish. In a second shallow dish, whisk the eggs. In a third shallow dish, mix together the Parmesan cheese, panko bread crumbs, traditional bread crumbs, Italian seasoning and garlic salt.

Trim the ends of the eggplant and cut the eggplant into strips that are 4 to 5 inches (10 to 13 cm) long and ½ inch (13 mm) thick.

Dip the eggplant fries into the flour, then the eggs, then the cheese and bread crumb mixture, coating them evenly.

Spray the air fryer basket with the spray oil and place a single layer of the eggplant fries into the basket. Spray them with the spray oil.

Air-fry the eggplant fries at 400°F (204°C) for 10 minutes, flipping the fries halfway through the cooking time. Repeat this process with the remaining eggplant fries.

Serve the eggplant fries warm with the marinara sauce for dipping.

MAKES:
6 SERVINGS

1 cup (120 g) all-purpose flour

2 large eggs

½ cup (90 g) grated Parmesan cheese

½ cup (28 g) panko bread crumbs

½ cup (60 g) traditional bread crumbs

1 tsp Italian seasoning

¾ tsp garlic salt

1 large eggplant

Spray oil

1 cup (240 ml) marinara sauce, to serve

GOAT CHEESE BITES

These tangy little Goat Cheese Bites are easy to make, they come together quickly and they are a great way to get a simple yet elegant appetizer on the table in no time. With just a few minutes and a few ingredients, these fabulous, crispy, creamy bites are ready to be drizzled with honey and served.

Line a large baking sheet with parchment paper.

Slice the goat cheese into 16 pieces and roll each piece into a ball.

Arrange three shallow bowls to form a breading station. Place the flour in the first bowl. Place the eggs in the second bowl. Place the panko bread crumbs in the third shallow bowl.

Coat each cheese ball in the flour, then dip it into the egg, then coat it in the panko bread crumbs.

Place the goat cheese balls on the prepared baking sheet and transfer the baking sheet to the freezer for about 10 minutes to allow the cheese to firm up.

Spray the air fryer basket with the spray oil and place a single layer of the goat cheese bites in the basket. Lightly spray the tops of the bites with the spray oil.

Air-fry the bites at 390°F (199°C) for 4 minutes. Remove the bites from the air fryer basket and serve them warm drizzled with the honey.

MAKES: 16 BITES

1 (10-oz [283-g]) log fresh goat cheese

1 cup (120 g) all-purpose flour

2 large eggs, beaten

2 cups (110 g) panko bread crumbs

Spray oil

Honey, to serve

TIP: These goat cheese bites are fabulous on top of a salad.

BACON-WRAPPED STEAK BITES

Steak and bacon come together to make one amazing appetizer. I am so glad I can make these in just minutes in my air fryer, because they disappear faster than any other appetizer on the table. I like to make these for holiday parties or special occasions because they are a bit decadent and perfect to make any get together a little more fabulous.

Cut the steak into bite-sized pieces. Sprinkle the pieces with the steak seasoning.

Cut the bacon slices in half and wrap a half slice around each steak bite.

Secure the bacon to the steak bites with toothpicks.

Place a single layer of steak bites in the air fryer basket. Air-fry the steak bites at 390°F (199°C) for 4 minutes. Flip the steak bites and air-fry them for another 4 minutes.

Check to see if the bites are done to your preference. If they are done to your liking, remove them from the air fryer basket.

TIP: These go great with a horseradish dipping sauce or your favorite steak sauce.

**MAKES:
2 TO 4 SERVINGS**

1 lb (454 g) petite sirloin steak or other quick-cooking, tender steak

Steak seasoning or rub (I recommend Montreal seasoning)

10 to 12 slices cooked bacon

GLAZED SPICY TURKEY PINWHEELS

I have been making these pinwheels for every birthday party, holiday or get-together for as long as I can remember. They are a family favorite. Of course, you know I had to try making them in the air fryer, and of course they came out perfect. I love that I can make our favorite snack without turning the oven on. Even better: These are totally customizable to your family's taste.

Unroll the crescent roll dough and separate it into 4 rectangles. Seal the perforations by pinching.

Divide the pepper Jack cheese and turkey evenly among the rectangles. Roll the rectangles up, starting at the shorter sides. Pinch the seams to seal. Cut each roll into six slices.

Place a parchment round in the bottom of the air fryer basket and place a single layer of the pinwheels in the basket, being careful not to overcrowd the pinwheels (you don't want them touching).

In a small bowl, mix together the butter, mustard and garlic salt. Brush the butter mixture over the pinwheels and sprinkle them with the poppy seeds.

Air-fry the pinwheels at 360°F (182°C) for 6 to 8 minutes. Repeat this process with the remaining pinwheels.

Serve the pinwheels warm.

MAKES: 24 PINWHEELS

1 (8-oz [227-g]) can crescent rolls

1 cup (112 g) shredded pepper Jack cheese

8 oz (227 g) sliced deli turkey

4 tbsp (60 g) butter, melted

1 tbsp (15 g) Dijon mustard

1/8 tsp garlic salt

1 tsp poppy seeds

TIP: Want a little more spice? Add some chopped jalapeños. Want no spice? Swap out the pepper Jack for Cheddar.

AVOCADO FRIES

Avocados are so popular right now and are popping up in everything from ice cream to smoothies. These avocado fries are crispy and creamy and great for dipping in your favorite sauce.

Arrange three shallow dishes to create a breading station. Place the flour in the first dish. In the second dish, beat together the eggs, water and hot sauce. In the third dish, mix together the panko bread crumbs, black pepper, garlic salt and cumin.

Dip the avocado wedges into the flour, shaking off the excess. Next, dip them into the egg mixture. Finally, coat them in the panko mixture, gently pressing the panko mixture onto the slices to be sure they are completely coated.

Spray the air fryer basket with the spray oil. Place the avocado slices in the air fryer in a single layer. Generously spray them with the spray oil.

Air-fry the avocado fries at 400°F (204°C) for 8 minutes, flipping them halfway through the cooking time, until they are golden and crispy. Repeat the process with the remaining avocado fries if needed.

Remove the avocado fries from the air fryer and serve them with your favorite dipping sauce.

MAKES:
4 SERVINGS

½ cup (120 g) all-purpose flour

2 large eggs

1 tbsp (15 ml) water

½ tbsp (8 ml) hot sauce

1 cup (55 g) panko bread crumbs

1 tsp black pepper

1 tsp garlic salt

¼ tsp ground cumin

2 small avocados, each cut into about 8 wedges

Spray oil

GARLIC-HERB JALAPEÑO POPPERS

Jalapeño poppers are a staple party snack, right? I've seen them made a million different ways and each way is delicious. But today we are going to make them in the air fryer and we're going to give them a little garlic-herb twist. These are simple to make with just a few ingredients, and they take mere minutes in the air fryer.

In a medium bowl, combine the cream cheese and Monterey Jack cheese and mix them well.

Place 1½ tablespoons (23 g) of the filling into each jalapeño half.

In a medium bowl, combine the crackers and paprika. Top each jalapeño half with a little of the cracker mixture.

Spray the air fryer basket with the spray oil. Place the poppers in the air fryer basket in a single layer. You may need to work in batches.

Air-fry the poppers at 350°F (177°C) for 10 minutes.

Serve the poppers with ranch dressing (if using).

TIP: You could switch out the jalapeño peppers for mini sweet peppers if you don't like spicy poppers.

MAKES: 24 POPPERS

8 oz (227 g) garlic-herb cream cheese, softened

½ cup (56 g) shredded Monterey Jack or mozzarella cheese

12 medium jalapeños, halved lengthwise and seeded

½ cup (120 g) buttery crackers, crushed

¼ tsp paprika

Spray oil

Ranch dressing, to serve (optional)

CRISPY GNOCCHI WITH PESTO

I love gnocchi, but have you ever had it crispy? They are full of next-level flavor and so addicting! I serve mine with pesto on the side, but you can use Alfredo or marinara as well.

In a large bowl, toss the gnocchi with the oil, garlic salt and black pepper. Place the gnocchi in the air fryer. Air-fry the gnocchi at 350°F (177°C) for 6 to 8 minutes, shaking the basket occasionally.

Open the air fryer and sprinkle the gnocchi with the Parmesan cheese. Air-fry the gnocchi for another 2 minutes.

Remove the gnocchi from the air fryer basket and serve it with the pesto.

MAKES:
4 SERVINGS

12 oz (340 g) refrigerated or frozen gnocchi

2 tbsp (30 ml) oil

¼ tsp garlic salt

¼ tsp black pepper

2 tbsp (22 g) grated Parmesan cheese

1 cup (240 ml) pesto

MINI CHICKEN–BACON–RANCH EGG ROLLS

I have found over the years that you can make anything with chicken, bacon and ranch and people will go crazy! So I put that combo in egg roll form where they get nice and crunchy in the air fryer. The perfect little snack!

In a large bowl, combine the chicken, bacon, ranch dressing, Colby Jack cheese and green onion.

Place 1 to 2 tablespoons (15 to 30 g) of the chicken filling in each egg roll wrapper.

Fold one corner of the egg roll wrapper to the middle. Fold each side in toward the middle. Roll the egg roll wrapper around the filling.

Spray the air fryer basket with the spray oil. Place a single layer of egg rolls, seam side down, in the air fryer basket. Spray the tops with the spray oil and sprinkle a little kosher salt on each egg roll.

Air-fry the egg rolls at 390°F (199°C) for 4 minutes. Flip the egg rolls and air-fry them for 4 more minutes.

Repeat this process with the remaining egg rolls.

Serve the egg rolls with extra ranch dressing for dipping.

MAKES:
16 EGG ROLLS

2 (4-oz [112-g]) boneless, skinless chicken breasts, cooked and shredded

12 slices bacon, cooked and crumbled

¼ cup (60 ml) ranch dressing, plus more to serve

1 cup (113 g) shredded Colby Jack cheese

1 tbsp (6 g) coarsely chopped green onion

16 square egg roll wrappers

Spray oil

Kosher salt

PULLED PORK POTATO SKINS

Pulled Pork Potato Skins are a great twist on classic potato skins. Barbecue sauce, crispy onions, melty cheese and delicious pork all come together in these amazing potato skins.

Wash and dry the potatoes. Coat each potato with the oil and sprinkle all sides with the salt.

Air-fry the potatoes at 380°F (193°C) for 30 minutes, flipping the potatoes halfway through the cooking time. Check them to see if they are easily pierced with a fork; if not, air-fry them in 2-minute increments until they are cooked through.

Let the potatoes cool slightly and cut them in half. Scoop out some of the potatoes' flesh, leaving the skin intact. Sprinkle each potato skin with additional salt and the black pepper.

In a medium bowl, mix together the pulled pork and barbecue sauce. Evenly divide the pulled pork among the potato skins. Top each potato skin with the Colby Jack cheese.

Air-fry the potato skins at 350°F (177°C) for 3 to 5 minutes, until the cheese is melted.

Remove the potato skins from the air fryer and top each one with the crispy fried onions.

MAKES: 6 SERVINGS

6 small baking potatoes

2 tbsp (30 ml) oil

Salt

Black pepper

2 cups (500 g) prepared pulled pork

¼ cup (60 ml) barbecue sauce

½ to ¾ cup (56 to 84 g) shredded Colby Jack cheese

3 tbsp (15 g) crispy fried onions

BACON-WRAPPED SAUSAGES

Salty, sweet and smoky, these Bacon-Wrapped Sausages are little bites of heaven. I swear that I could triple this recipe and it would still not be enough for parties.

Wrap each sausage with a third of a slice of bacon. Use a toothpick to secure the bacon.

Place a parchment round in the bottom of the air fryer. Place a single layer of the bacon-wrapped sausages in the air fryer.

Sprinkle a little brown sugar on the bacon on each sausage.

Air-fry the sausages at 360°F (182°C) for 8 minutes.

**MAKES:
6 TO 8 SERVINGS**

1 (12- to 14-oz [340- to 397-g]) package cocktail sausages

12 to 15 slices precooked microwavable bacon, cut into thirds

½ cup (72 g) brown sugar

HONEY MUSTARD—GLAZED PIGS IN A BLANKET

Pigs in a blanket are the quintessential party food. I honestly cannot make enough of them for parties—they disappear in minutes. I am so glad I can make them in the air fryer, because that means I don't have to turn on my oven during parties (it gets so hot with all those extra people in the house). I also make a fancy glaze to go on top to take these regular pigs in a blanket over the top!

Lay a parchment round in the bottom of the air fryer.

Cut each triangle of crescent dough into three strips and roll each of the sausages in one strip of dough and place each one in the air fryer. You will need to work in batches.

In a small bowl, combine the butter, honey, mustard, onion powder, Worcestershire sauce, poppy seeds and brown sugar.

Brush the butter glaze over all the pigs in a blanket.

Air-fry the pigs in a blanket at 325°F (163°C) for 6 to 8 minutes.

MAKES:
24 SERVINGS

1 (8-oz [227-g]) can crescent rolls

1 (14-oz [397-g]) package cocktail sausages

¼ cup (60 g) butter, melted

1 tbsp (15 ml) honey

1 tbsp (15 g) Dijon mustard

½ tsp onion powder

¼ tsp Worcestershire sauce

½ tbsp (4 g) poppy seeds

2 tbsp (18 g) brown sugar

ROASTED RED PEPPER HUMMUS WITH BAKED PITA CHIPS

Hummus from an air fryer? Kind of! We are going to use the air fryer to roast the red pepper for the hummus, and we are going to make some delicious pita chips in the air fryer while we blend up our easy roasted red pepper hummus.

Spritz the red bell pepper with the spray oil. Place the bell pepper in the air fryer and air-fry it at 400°F (204°C) for 20 minutes, flipping it halfway through the cooking time.

Remove the pepper from the air fryer and let it cool for about 20 minutes. Wipe off most of the charred skin with a paper towel, then cut off the top and scoop out the seeds.

In a food processer, combine the bell pepper, garlic, chickpeas, tahini, lemon juice, salt and black pepper. Process until the hummus is smooth.

Cut each of the pita breads into eighths.

Spray the air fryer basket with the spray oil and place a single layer of pita chips in the air fryer. Spritz them with spray oil and sprinkle them with salt.

Air-fry the pita chips at 350°F (177°C) for 4 minutes. Repeat this process with the remaining pita breads.

Serve the pita chips with the hummus.

MAKES: 4 SERVINGS

1 small red bell pepper

Spray oil

2 cloves garlic, coarsely chopped

1 (15-oz [420-g]) can chickpeas, drained

2 tbsp (30 g) tahini

1 tbsp (15 ml) fresh lemon juice

⅛ tsp salt, plus more as needed

⅛ tsp black pepper

4 pita breads

BEAN CAKE SLIDERS

My grandma makes the best bean cake sandwiches, and this is my take on that delicious recipe. I make these small, crisp them in my air fryer and serve them as appetizers. They are a great alternative to all your usual appetizers. The crispy bean cake, bite of onion and soft bun all make for an amazing slider.

In a large bowl, thoroughly mash the beans. Add the bacon, salt, black pepper and Cajun seasoning.

Add the flour in ½-cup (60-g) increments, until it is thick enough to create patties.

Form the bean mixture into 8 small patties.

Spray the bottom of the air fryer with the spray oil. Place the patties in the air fryer and spray the tops generously with the spray oil so there are no dry patches of flour anywhere.

Air-fry the patties at 370°F (188°C) for 5 minutes.

Flip the patties over carefully and add a slice of onion to each one.

Air-fry the patties for another 5 minutes.

Spread each bun with mayonnaise and add a bean patty to each one.

MAKES:
4 SERVINGS

3 cups (525 g) white northern beans, drained

3 slices bacon, cooked and crumbled

1 tsp salt

½ tsp black pepper

¼ tsp Cajun seasoning

1 to 1½ cups (120 to 180 g) all-purpose flour, plus more if needed

Spray oil

1 small onion, thinly sliced

8 soft slider buns

Mayonnaise

RISE AND SHINE

We all know that breakfast is the most important meal of the day, but it is often the most rushed. Who has time to make breakfast in the hustle and bustle of trying to get out the door for work and school? Not me, that's for sure.

On those crazy mornings, I need something quick—and that is where my trusty air fryer comes in. My air fryer makes breakfast in no time: biscuits ready in minutes, egg bites better than any coffee place can whip up and, of course, cinnamon rolls my whole family loves made without spending hours in the kitchen.

You can create amazing breakfast dishes right in your air fryer, and they will be ready long before the kids rush out to the school bus. So put away your cereal bowls and get ready to create some filling, warm breakfast recipes for your family!

AIR FRYER RAINBOW BAGELS

Have you guys seen those amazing rainbow bagels? They look awesome! I wanted to re-create them at home, but all that time spent letting the dough rise and boiling the bagels before baking was just too much for me! I found out I could make bagels right in my trusty air fryer with only four ingredients: self-rising flour, Greek yogurt and food coloring is all you need to make these gorgeous bagels (and a quick egg wash makes them shiny). In no time you can have these colorful beauties on your breakfast table.

Arrange four medium bowls on a work surface. In each of the bowls, mix together 1 cup (120 g) of the flour with 1 cup (285 g) of the Greek yogurt and a few drops of one of the food colorings. Mix until all the ingredients in each bowl are combined.

Dust the work surface with flour. On the work surface, roll each color of dough into a ball and slice each ball into 16 pieces.

Take 1 piece of dough from each color and twist the 4 pieces together to form a ring. Repeat this process until you have no more dough left.

Brush the tops of each bagel with the beaten eggs.

Place a parchment round in the air fryer. Place 2 bagels in the air fryer basket and air fry them at 330°F (166°C) for 10 minutes. Repeat this process until all the bagels are cooked.

TIP: You can leave out the food coloring for plain bagels, or you can use this recipe and add your favorite toppings or flavors.

MAKES:
16 BAGELS

4 cups (480 g) self-rising flour, plus more as needed

4 cups (1.1 kg) plain fat-free Greek yogurt

4 bottles food coloring

2 large eggs, beaten

APPLE CIDER FRENCH TOAST STICKS

The first thing I ever made in my air fryer was frozen French toast sticks. They came out amazingly well, and that was when I fell in love with my air fryer. I wanted to make some of my own French toast sticks, since they are my kids' favorite breakfast. I love these Apple Cider French Toast Sticks—they are perfect for dunking in maple syrup.

In a shallow dish, mix together the eggs, milk, 1 tablespoon (7 g) of the apple cider mix, butter, vanilla and cinnamon.

Place a parchment round in the air fryer.

Quickly dunk each strip of bread into the egg mixture and place a single layer of the French toast sticks in the air fryer, making sure they don't touch.

Air-fry the French toast sticks at 370°F (188°C) for 5 minutes. Flip the sticks and air-fry them for 3 to 4 minutes, until they are brown. Repeat this process with the remaining French toast sticks.

In a small bowl, mix together the sugar and remaining 1 tablespoon (7 g) of apple cider mix. Sprinkle this mixture on the warm French toast sticks.

Serve the French toast sticks with the maple syrup.

TIP: You can also serve these dusted with powdered sugar.

MAKES: 4 SERVINGS

2 large eggs

⅓ cup (80 ml) milk

2 tbsp (14 g) powdered apple cider mix, divided

1 tbsp (15 g) butter, melted

1 tsp pure vanilla extract

½ tsp ground cinnamon

4 thick slices bread, cut into thirds

2 tbsp (24 g) sugar

Pure maple syrup, to serve

MINI CHEESY BREAKFAST PIZZAS

This is one of my family's favorite quick breakfasts. These breakfast pizzas are customizable to each person's tastes. They are portable, making them great for that school drop-off line. They can be prepped in just minutes and come out of the air fryer warm and cheesy. Keep the ingredients to make these on hand and you are never more than a few minutes away from a quick, delicious breakfast.

In a medium skillet over medium-low heat, melt the butter.

In a medium bowl, whisk together the eggs, salt and black pepper. Add the eggs to the skillet and cook them for 3 to 5 minutes, until they are just set.

Meanwhile, split the English muffins in half.

Top each muffin half with a quarter of the mozzarella cheese. Divide the scrambled eggs among the muffin halves. Top each with the Cheddar cheese. Finally, top the pizzas with the toppings of your choice.

Place the English muffin pizzas in the air fryer and air-fry them at 400°F (204°C) for 4 minutes.

MAKES: 4 PIZZAS

1 tbsp (15 g) butter

5 large eggs

Salt

Black pepper

2 English muffins

½ cup (56 g) shredded mozzarella cheese

½ cup (60 g) shredded Cheddar cheese

Toppings of choice, as needed (e.g., mini pepperoni, crumbled bacon, black olives, spinach)

PUMPKIN-MAPLE POP-TARTS

Pop-Tarts are a busy-morning breakfast staple. But I wanted to make some myself and skip some of those sugar bombs first thing in the morning. These Pumpkin-Maple Pop-Tarts come together in minutes and are delicious warm out of the air fryer.

MAKES: 6 POP-TARTS

2 refrigerated premade pie dough crusts

1 cup (245 g) pumpkin puree

1/3 cup (48 g) brown sugar

1 tsp pumpkin pie spice

1/2 tsp ground cinnamon

1 to 1 1/4 cups (130 to 163 g) powdered sugar, plus more as needed

1 tbsp (15 ml) milk

2 tbsp (30 ml) pure maple syrup

On a floured work surface, roll out 1 pie crust and cut 6 equal rectangles out of the dough. Repeat this process with the second piece of dough.

In a small bowl, mix together the pumpkin puree, brown sugar, pumpkin pie spice and cinnamon until the ingredients are well blended.

Put 2 tablespoons (30 g) of the filling on 6 of the rectangles and gently spread the filling to cover the rectangles, leaving a generous edge of dough around the filling.

Top each of the rectangles with filling with one of the plain rectangles.

Fold over each rectangle and using a fork, crimp three edges around each pop-tart. Use a toothpick to poke a few holes in the top of the pop-tart.

Place 2 to 3 pop-tarts in the air fryer and air-fry them at 350°F (177°C) for 10 minutes.

Repeat this process with the remaining pop-tarts until they are all baked.

Transfer the air-fried pop-tarts to a cooling rack.

In a small bowl, combine the powdered sugar, milk and maple syrup. If the glaze is too thin, add a little more powdered sugar.

Spoon the glaze over the pop-tarts and let the glaze harden before serving.

BREAKFAST CHIMICHANGAS

These warm, hearty, crispy Breakfast Chimichangas are out of this world. Filled with flavorful ingredients like peppers, onion, chorizo, eggs and salsa, these are sure to wake up you and your taste buds in the morning.

MAKES:
4 CHIMICHANGAS

1 cup (140 g) ground chorizo

1 cup (175 g) frozen mixed bell peppers and onions

8 large eggs

Salt

Black pepper

¼ cup (64 g) salsa

4 (10-inch [25-cm]) tortillas

1 cup (112 g) shredded Colby Jack cheese

Spray oil

Sour cream, to serve

In a large skillet over medium heat, cook the chorizo for 8 to 10 minutes, crumbling it with a wooden spoon as it cooks. When the chorizo is brown, transfer it to paper towels to drain.

Add the bell peppers and onions to the skillet and cook them for about 5 minutes, until the onions are translucent. Remove the bell peppers and onions from the skillet.

Reduce the heat to medium-low.

In a medium bowl, whisk the eggs with the salt and black pepper. Add the eggs to the skillet and scramble them for 3 to 5 minutes, until they have just set.

Spread 1 tablespoon (16 g) of the salsa on each of the tortillas. Add one-fourth of the chorizo and one-fourth of the bell peppers and onions to each tortilla.

Divide the scrambled eggs among the 4 tortillas and top each one evenly with the Colby Jack cheese.

Fold in two sides of each tortilla and then roll it up all the way.

Spray the inside of the air fryer basket with the spray oil.

Place two chimichangas, seam side down, in the air fryer basket. Spray the tops of the chimichangas with the spray oil.

Air-fry the chimichangas at 400°F (204°C) for 8 minutes. Repeat this process with the other two chimichangas.

Serve the chimichangas with the sour cream.

TIP: Add jalapeños or green chilis if you want a little more kick.

LOADED HASH BROWN PATTIES

There is nothing I love more than a good hash brown. In the air fryer, hash browns are crispy and perfect. There's not much else you can do to improve them—except add some of your other morning favorites on top to make the ultimate breakfast.

Air-fry the hash brown patties at 400°F (204°C) for 10 minutes, flipping them halfway through the cooking time.

While the hash brown patties are cooking, melt the butter in a medium skillet over medium-low heat. Whisk together your eggs, salt and black pepper in a medium bowl. Add the eggs to the skillet and scramble them for 3 to 5 minutes, until they have just set.

Pull out the basket from the air fryer and carefully top each of the hash brown patties with an equal amount of the scrambled eggs.

Crumble 2 slices of the bacon on top of each hash brown patty. Sprinkle some Cheddar cheese on top of each hash brown patty.

Put the basket back in the air fryer and air-fry the loaded hash brown patties at 400°F (204°C) for 2 minutes, just until the cheese is melted.

Remove the hash brown patties from the air fryer and sprinkle them with the green onion.

MAKES: 4 SERVINGS

4 frozen hash brown patties

1 tbsp (15 g) butter

4 large eggs

Salt

Black pepper

8 slices bacon, cooked and crumbled

¾ cup (90 g) shredded Cheddar cheese

1 tbsp (6 g) coarsely chopped green onion

STEAK FAJITA HASH

I love a good plate of sizzling steak fajitas, and I also love a great steak hash with potatoes and onions. So of course this Steak Fajita Hash is the best of both worlds in one easy-to-make, delicious dish.

Preheat the air fryer at 400°F (204°C) for 5 minutes.

Meanwhile, season the steak with ½ tablespoon (4 g) of the fajita seasoning. Add the steak to the air fryer basket and air-fry it at 400°F (204°C) for 5 minutes. Flip the steak and air-fry it for 3 minutes.

Remove the steak from the air fryer and let the meat rest.

Place a parchment round in the bottom of the air fryer basket.

Place the potatoes and bell peppers and onions in the air fryer basket. Sprinkle the potatoes with the remaining ½ tablespoon (5 g) of fajita seasoning. Cook the vegetables at 400°F (204°C) for 8 minutes, flipping the vegetables and shaking the basket halfway through the cooking time.

Cut the steak into small pieces and add them to the potatoes.

Divide the hash between two plates. Garnish each serving with the salsa, sour cream and guacamole.

TIP: You can use leftover steak or chicken for this recipe.

MAKES: 2 SERVINGS

1 large ribeye steak or other tender steak

1 tbsp (9 g) fajita seasoning, divided

2 cups (450 g) diced yellow potatoes

1 cup (175 g) frozen mixed bell peppers and onions

Salsa, to serve

Sour cream, to serve

Guacamole, to serve

SPICY SPINACH EGG BITES

Egg bites are all the rage right now. These fluffy little bites of egg became popular in that famous coffee shop, and now they are everywhere! For good reason too—they are so delicious, and you can customize them with the flavors you like. These whip up in minutes and cook in no time. They are a great protein-packed breakfast.

Note that you need a silicone egg bite mold for this recipe. They are very inexpensive on Amazon. You can use silicone muffin cups in a pinch.

In a medium bowl, whisk together the eggs, cottage cheese and milk. Add the spinach, jalapeños, salt, black pepper and Cheddar cheese.

Spray the silicone egg bite mold with the spray oil. Fill the molds with the egg mixture, but do not fill them all the way to the top—leave a little room for them to expand.

Air-fry the egg bites at 380°F (193°C) for 10 minutes.

Let the egg bites cool slightly and then turn them out onto a plate.

TIP: Store the egg bites in a ziplock bag in the freezer. These freeze well!

MAKES: 12 TO 14 BITES

4 large eggs

½ cup (115 g) cottage cheese

¼ cup (60 ml) milk

¼ cup (45 g) cooked and drained spinach

1 tbsp (11 g) diced jalapeños

½ tsp salt

¼ tsp black pepper

½ cup (60 g) shredded Cheddar cheese

Spray oil

RASPBERRY DANISH

I love these Raspberry Danishes so much. They are great for brunch or a holiday breakfast. They also make a wonderful snack or dessert any time of day. These are so easy to make—they come together in just minutes and cook up just as fast!

Unroll the crescent roll dough on a work surface. Press two crescent triangles together to make a rectangle and fold over the edges slightly to create a small edge.

In a medium bowl, mix together the cream cheese and powdered sugar until they are well combined. Spread one-fourth of the cream cheese mixture onto each rectangle.

Divide the raspberry jam among the four rectangles and spread the jam over the top of the cream cheese.

Sprinkle a touch of additional powdered sugar around the edges of each Danish.

Place two Danishes in the air fryer basket. Air-fry the Danishes at 350°F (177°C) for 5 to 6 minutes. Repeat this process with the remaining Danishes.

Let the Danishes cool slightly before serving.

TIP: You can swap out the raspberry jam for your favorite variety.

MAKES:
4 SERVINGS

1 (8-oz [224-g]) can crescent rolls

8 oz (227 g) cream cheese, softened

2 tbsp (16 g) powdered sugar, plus more as needed

½ cup (160 g) raspberry jam

MAPLE SAUSAGE BALLS

My family loves sausage balls. They are a staple every year for Christmas breakfast. My sister and I love dipping them in syrup, so I figured I could change up my usual recipe to get some syrup flavor into the sausage balls—they were perfect. These are a great addition to any breakfast or brunch. They even make a fabulous snack!

In a large bowl, combine the sausage, Cheddar cheese, pancake mix and maple syrup. Stir with a wooden spoon until the ingredients are mixed thoroughly.

Using a small scoop, roll the mixture into balls. (If you don't have a scoop, just roll the mixture into evenly sized balls.)

Place the sausage balls in the air fryer basket in a single layer with a little space between each one. Air-fry the sausage balls at 370°F (188°C) for 6 minutes. Repeat this process with the remaining sausage balls.

MAKES:
48 TO 60 BALLS

1 lb (454 g) maple pork sausage

4 cups (480 g) shredded mild Cheddar cheese

3 cups (390 g) pancake mix

1 tbsp (15 ml) pure maple syrup

PUMPKIN-BANANA MUFFINS

Banana muffins are my go-to when I have some brown bananas hanging around. But I wanted to see if I could make muffins in the air fryer, so I used my recipe for moist banana muffins; just to be sure they stayed moist, I substituted some of the banana for pumpkin puree. What a delicious experiment! Make a batch of these in the beginning of the week and you will have a quick, tasty breakfast all week (if they last that long).

In a large bowl, combine the bananas, pumpkin puree, granulated sugar and brown sugar. Use a hand mixer to beat the ingredients together until they are combined. Beat in the butter, oil, eggs and vanilla until combined.

Add the flour, baking soda, cinnamon and salt, mixing by hand to avoid overmixing the batter.

Spray 12 silicone muffin liners with the spray oil. Fill the liners three-fourths of the way with batter.

Place six of the muffins in the air fryer. Air-fry the muffins at 320°F (160°C) for 10 minutes.

Insert a toothpick into the centers of the muffins. If the toothpick comes out clean, the muffins are cooked through. If the toothpick does not come out clean, air-fry the muffins for 2 minutes and check again. Repeat this process with the remaining muffins.

Let the muffins cool before serving.

TIP: Feel free to add some walnuts or chocolate chips to your muffins!

MAKES:
12 MUFFINS

2 small, ripe bananas

1 cup (245 g) pumpkin puree

½ cup (96 g) granulated sugar

½ cup (72 g) brown sugar

6 tbsp (90 g) unsalted butter, melted

6 tbsp (90 ml) vegetable or canola oil

2 large eggs

1 tsp pure vanilla extract

2 cups (240 g) all purpose flour

2 tsp (8 g) baking soda

2 tsp (6 g) ground cinnamon

¼ tsp salt

Spray oil

BREAKFAST GRILLED CHEESE

Is there anything better than a comforting grilled cheese to start the day? Add some sausage and egg to that and you have a winner. This Breakfast Grilled Cheese is a cinch to make and so yummy. I use frozen cooked sausage patties to make my morning even easier—plus, they are the perfect size for a grilled cheese sandwich.

In a large skillet over medium heat, cook the sausage patties for 5 to 8 minutes, until they have browned. Remove the sausage patties from the skillet and set them aside. Place the skillet back over medium heat. Add 2 tablespoons (30 g) of the butter to the skillet and allow it to melt.

Carefully crack the eggs into the skillet, ensuring that the yolks don't break. Season the eggs with the salt and black pepper. Cook the eggs for 3 to 5 minutes, until the yolks are just set. Remove the eggs from the skillet and set them aside.

Butter one side of each slice of bread with the remaining 4 tablespoons (60 g) of butter. Lay 2 slices of bread, buttered side down, in the air fryer basket. Add a slice of Cheddar cheese to each piece of bread in the basket.

Add a sausage patty, egg and slice of American cheese on top of the Cheddar cheese.

Top the American cheese with another slice of the buttered bread, buttered side up.

Air-fry the sandwiches at 370°F (188°C) for 4 minutes. Flip the sandwiches carefully and air-fry them for another 4 minutes.

Remove the grilled cheese sandwiches from the air fryer and repeat this process with the other two sandwiches. Serve the sandwiches hot.

MAKES:
4 SERVINGS

4 frozen sausage patties

6 tbsp (90 g) butter, softened, divided

4 large eggs

Salt

Black pepper

8 slices bread

4 slices Cheddar cheese

4 slices American cheese

BACON—PEPPER JACK EGG BITES

Here is another great variation of those delicious egg bites, this time with bacon. These get a little kick from pepper Jack cheese and are so addictive. One or two of these make a filling, quick breakfast.

In a medium bowl, whisk together the eggs, cottage cheese and milk. Add the bacon, salt, black pepper and pepper Jack cheese, whisking to combine.

Spray 12 to 14 silicone egg bite molds with the spray oil. Fill the molds with the egg mixture, but do not fill them all the way to the top—leave a little room for them to expand.

Air-fry the egg bites at 380°F (193°C) for 10 minutes.

Let the egg bites cool slightly and then turn them out onto a plate.

**MAKES:
12 TO 14 BITES**

4 large eggs

½ cup (115 g) cottage cheese

¼ cup (60 ml) milk

8 slices bacon, cooked and crumbled

½ tsp salt

¼ tsp black pepper

½ cup (56 g) shredded pepper Jack cheese

Spray oil

CARAMEL APPLE CINNAMON ROLLS

Did you know you can make soft, fluffy, ooey-gooey cinnamon rolls in the air fryer? Air-frying cinnamon rolls is much faster than baking them—there's no preheating the oven! I make a quick caramel apple topping for these to really put them over the top.

In a medium saucepan over medium heat, melt the butter. Add the apple, cinnamon and brown sugar. Cook this mixture for 8 to 10 minutes, until the apple is tender.

Spray an 8-inch (20-cm) cake pan with the spray oil. Place the cinnamon rolls in the prepared cake pan and pour the apple mixture over the top of the rolls.

Air-fry the cinnamon rolls at 350°F (177°C) for 9 to 10 minutes. Remove the pan from the air fryer basket carefully.

While the cinnamon rolls are still warm, drizzle the cinnamon rolls with their icing and the caramel sauce. Serve the cinnamon rolls warm.

TIP: If you prefer not to use the cinnamon rolls' icing, you can skip it and just use the caramel sauce.

MAKES: 8 SERVINGS

2 tbsp (30 g) butter

1 small apple, finely chopped

½ tsp ground cinnamon

1 tbsp (9 g) brown sugar

Spray oil

1 (12-oz [336-g]) can cinnamon rolls with icing

¼ cup (60 ml) caramel sauce

HAM AND CHEDDAR EGG CROISSANTS

One of my most popular recipes is my ham and cheese croissants. I decided to throw an egg on them and make them a breakfast item. I love the fact that these are individually wrapped—that makes them perfect for grabbing on my way out the door.

In a large skillet over medium heat, melt the butter. Carefully crack the eggs into the skillet and season them with the salt and black pepper. Cook the eggs for 3 to 5 minutes, until the yolks are set.

Lay out four squares of foil large enough to wrap up the croissants. Place the bottom of each croissant on a piece of foil.

Lay a slice of Cheddar cheese, 2 slices of ham, 1 egg and another slice of Cheddar cheese on the bottom of each croissant. Place the top half of the croissant on the sandwich and wrap it in the foil.

Place two of the sandwiches in the air fryer. Air-fry them at 350°F (177°C) for 8 to 10 minutes. Repeat this process with the remaining sandwiches.

Serve the sandwiches warm.

TIP: Swap out the Cheddar cheese for your favorite kind.

MAKES: 4 SERVINGS

2 tbsp (30 g) butter

4 large eggs

Salt

Black pepper

4 croissants, cut in half

8 slices Cheddar cheese

8 slices deli ham

DOUGHNUTS THREE WAYS

You can make fresh doughnuts in your air fryer in less than twenty minutes, which means you can make your family hot doughnuts before work. That's crazy! I include three different frosting and topping options so you can have your favorite. Each of the topping recipes will cover a full batch of doughnuts.

To make the doughnuts, place a parchment round in the air fryer basket.

Cut a small circle out of the middle of each biscuit using a biscuit cutter or plastic bottle cap. Save the middles for doughnut holes.

Lay two to four doughnuts in the air fryer. Air-fry the doughnuts at 350°F (177°C) for 6 minutes, flipping them halfway through the cooking time. Repeat this process with the remaining doughnuts. To make doughnut holes, air-fry the doughnut holes at 350°F (177°C) for about 4 minutes.

While the doughnuts are cooking, prepare the toppings.

To make the chocolate glaze, whisk together the powdered sugar, cocoa powder, milk and vanilla in a medium bowl until the glaze is smooth. Dip one side of the doughnuts into the glaze and let it harden on the doughnut before serving.

To make the original glaze, mix together the milk, powdered sugar and corn syrup in a large microwave-safe bowl. Microwave the mixture for 30 seconds. Quickly dip both sides of the doughnuts into the glaze and place them on a baking rack to allow the glaze to set up before serving.

To make the cinnamon sugar, mix together the cinnamon and sugar in a medium bowl. Place the butter in another medium bowl. Dip both sides of the doughnuts in the butter and then coat them in the cinnamon sugar.

MAKES: 16 DOUGHNUTS

Doughnuts
2 (1-lb [454-g]) cans jumbo biscuits

Chocolate Glaze
1½ cups (195 g) powdered sugar

4 tbsp (28 g) unsweetened cocoa powder

2 tbsp (30 ml) milk

2 tsp (10 ml) pure vanilla extract

Original Glaze
½ cup (120 ml) milk

5 cups (650 g) powdered sugar

½ cup (120 ml) corn syrup

Cinnamon Sugar
2 tbsp (18 g) ground cinnamon

1 cup (192 g) granulated sugar

6 tbsp (90 g) butter, melted

TIP: While the glaze is still wet you can add sprinkles, coconut, chocolate chips—anything you like!

PECAN-PUMPKIN GRANOLA

I love to make a big batch of granola to have on hand all week. It makes the perfect quick breakfast with milk, a fantastic topping for oatmeal or yogurt and a convenient after-school snack. This granola recipe has all the warm flavors of pumpkin pie and a satisfying crunch from pumpkin seeds. It is so good!

Place a parchment round in the air fryer basket.

In a large bowl, mix together the oats, pecans and pumpkin seeds.

In a small bowl, mix together the oil, honey and pumpkin pie spice.

Pour the honey mixture over the oat mixture and stir until everything is coated.

Pour all the granola into the air fryer basket and air-fry the granola at 250°F (121°C) for 30 minutes, stirring often.

While the granola is air-frying, line a large baking sheet with parchment paper. Transfer the granola to the parchment paper and spread the granola into a single layer. Let it cool for 30 minutes.

TIP: Dried cranberries would be a great addition to this!

MAKES:
4 SERVINGS

1½ cups (120 g) rolled oats

1 cup (120 g) raw pecans

1 cup (200 g) raw pumpkin seeds

1 tbsp (15 ml) oil of choice

¼ cup (60 ml) honey or pure maple syrup

1 tsp pumpkin pie spice

SAUSAGE AND GRAVY HASH BROWN CASSEROLE

Being a good southern girl, I know how to make sausage gravy and biscuits, and I make it often. The dish is a go-to, especially when we have breakfast for dinner. I also love hash browns—potatoes are my weakness. I was making a big breakfast the other day and I got the idea to combine my sausage gravy with hash browns and have the best of both worlds. Of course, I popped it in my air fryer. For this recipe, you need a deep pan that fits inside your air fryer. I used the deep, square one I got from Amazon.

In a medium skillet over medium heat, cook the sausage for 8 to 10 minutes, breaking it apart as it cooks, until it is browned.

Meanwhile, put the hash browns in the air fryer and spray them lightly with the spray oil. Air-fry the hash browns at 370°F (188°C) for 7 minutes. Stir and flip the hash browns and air-fry them for 7 minutes.

Add the flour to the sausage and cook for 1 minute, stirring the flour into the sausage. Season the sausage with the salt and black pepper.

Add the milk to the sausage and increase the heat to medium-high. Stir the mixture with a wooden spoon, making sure to scrape the bottom of the skillet to loosen the brown bits. Bring the gravy to a bubble and cook it for 3 to 5 minutes, until it has thickened.

When the hash browns are done, transfer them to a deep 7- to 8-inch (18- to 20-cm) air fryer pan and pour the sausage gravy over the top of the hash browns.

(Because air fryers vary in size, their pans will vary in size; you may have to use two pans.) Put the pan in the air fryer and air-fry the casserole at 400°F (204°C) for 4 minutes.

Carefully remove the pan from the air fryer and let the casserole cool slightly before serving.

MAKES: 4 SERVINGS

1 lb (454 g) breakfast sausage of choice

4 cups (840 g) frozen shredded hash browns

Spray oil

1 tbsp (8 g) all-purpose flour

Salt

Black pepper

2 cups (480 ml) milk

BANANA PUDDING—STUFFED FRENCH TOAST

My mom loves banana pudding. When I was trying to come up with an over-the-top stuffed French toast recipe, I thought of banana pudding and put it all together. Filled with vanilla pudding and fresh bananas, this French toast is definitely a step up from your normal breakfast fare. This recipe works best if you buy a loaf of bread and slice it yourself, so that you can get some thick slices to stuff.

Place a parchment round in the air fryer basket and spray it lightly with the spray oil.

Slice 4 to 6 slices of bread that are 1½ to 2 inches (4 to 5 cm) thick. Slice each piece of bread roughly halfway from top to bottom, being careful not to cut all the way through the bread. This will form the pocket that holds the filling.

In a medium bowl, mix together the vanilla pudding and 1½ cups (360 ml) of the milk. Place the pudding in the fridge for about 5 minutes to allow it to thicken. When the pudding has thickened, it is time to assemble the stuffed French toast.

Put a few banana slices in the pocket of each slice of bread. Next, put some of the vanilla pudding in the pocket, but do not overstuff it with pudding. Finally, add a few more banana slices.

In a shallow dish, whisk together the remaining 1 cup (240 ml) of milk, eggs and vanilla. Dip each slice of French toast into the egg mixture and flip it over, making sure both sides are completely coated.

Put one or two slices of French toast in the air fryer basket. Air-fry the French toast at 350°F (177°C) for 10 minutes. Repeat this process with the remaining French toast.

Serve the French toast with the maple syrup, powdered sugar or whipped cream and plenty of sliced bananas.

MAKES: 4 TO 6 SERVINGS

Spray oil

1 loaf unsliced brioche or challah bread

1 (3-oz [85-g]) box instant vanilla pudding

2½ cups (600 ml) milk, divided

2 small bananas, thinly sliced, plus more to serve

2 large eggs

1 tsp pure vanilla extract

Pure maple syrup, to serve

Powdered sugar, to serve

Whipped cream, to serve

DENVER OMELET—STUFFED PEPPERS

When I was younger, I always wanted my grandma to make me omelets. They just seemed so fancy. One of the most popular omelets is a Denver omelet, which is usually full of cheese, ham and peppers. I thought, "Why not create that inside a pepper and make it in the air fryer?" So that is what I did! These come together quickly and are perfect for brunch or breakfast—they even make a great dinner.

In a medium bowl, whisk together the eggs, cream, salt and black pepper.

Slice the tops off the bell peppers and pull out the seeds and membranes. Divide the Cheddar cheese, ham and diced bell peppers among the 4 bell peppers. Pour the egg mixture into each bell pepper, filling it about three-fourths full. Give the mixture in each bell pepper a little stir to make sure everything is mixed.

Place all the bell peppers in the air fryer, making sure they are stable. Air-fry the stuffed peppers at 350°F (177°C) for 25 minutes. Insert a toothpick into the center of each stuffed pepper. If the toothpick comes out clean, the peppers are ready to serve.

TIP: You can cut the peppers in half lengthwise and lay them down before filling and cooking them.

MAKES: 4 SERVINGS

8 large eggs

1 tbsp (15 ml) heavy cream

½ tsp salt

¼ tsp black pepper

4 small bell peppers (any color)

¾ cup (90 g) shredded Cheddar cheese

¾ cup (113 g) diced ham

¾ cup (131 g) diced bell peppers (any color)

THE BEST BREAKFAST BURRITO

The breakfast burrito is a classic morning staple. My family loves them, everyone loves them! They are portable, customizable and freezer-friendly. They are also air fryer–friendly. I make them ahead of time and wrap them in foil—anytime someone needs a quick breakfast, they just pop a burrito in the air fryer, still wrapped in the foil, and they have a filling breakfast ready in minutes.

In a medium skillet over medium heat, warm the sausage until it is heated through. Remove it from the skillet. Return the skillet to medium heat.

In a medium bowl, whisk together the eggs, green onion, salt and black pepper. Melt the butter in the skillet and add the eggs. Scramble the eggs for 3 to 5 minutes, until they are just set.

Lay out the tortillas and spread 1 tablespoon (15 ml) of the queso cheese dip on each tortilla.

Add one-fourth of the sausage mixture to each tortilla. Add one-fourth of the egg mixture to each tortilla.

Divide the Cheddar cheese among the tortillas. Put 1 tablespoon (15 ml) of the salsa in each tortilla.

Fold the sides of each burrito in, and then roll up the burrito lengthwise. Wrap each burrito in foil.

Air-fry the wrapped burritos two or three at a time at 400°F (204°C) for 8 minutes. Repeat this process with the remaining burritos.

TIP: Swap the sausage for bacon or ham. Add jalapeños for a spicy bite.

MAKES: 4 SERVINGS

1 cup (140 g) cooked and crumbled breakfast sausage of choice

6 large eggs

1 tbsp (6 g) coarsely chopped green onion

Salt, as needed

Black pepper, as needed

1 tbsp (15 g) butter

4 (10-inch [25-cm]) tortillas

¼ cup (60 ml) queso cheese dip

¾ cup (90 g) shredded Cheddar cheese

¼ cup (60 ml) salsa

CRANBERRY–MUSTARD SAUSAGE BOMBS

These Cranberry-Mustard Sausage Bombs are definitely a little different than your normal breakfast fare—but oh my, are they delicious. Flavorful sausage is paired with a sweet and savory cranberry mustard and then wrapped in flaky biscuit dough. I pop these into my air fryer and they are done in no time.

Line the air fryer basket with a parchment round.

Roll the sausage into 16 equal balls.

Place the sausage balls in the air fryer basket and air-fry them at 400°F (204°C) for 10 to 12 minutes, until the sausage is cooked through.

Meanwhile, in a medium bowl, mix together the cranberry sauce, mustard and brown sugar until they are well combined.

Split each of the uncooked biscuits in half and spread a little of the cranberry mixture on each biscuit half.

Place one sausage ball on each biscuit half and enclose the sausage ball in the dough. Roll the dough into a ball.

Place eight sausage bombs in the air fryer basket with space between them. Sprinkle a few poppy seeds (if using) on the top of each one.

Air-fry the sausage bombs at 350°F (177°C) for 4 to 6 minutes, until the biscuit dough is cooked through. Repeat with the remaining sausage bombs.

MAKES:
16 SAUSAGE BOMBS

1 lb (454 g) breakfast sausage

1 cup (280 g) cranberry sauce

1 tbsp (15 g) Dijon mustard

½ tbsp (5 g) brown sugar

1 (1-lb [454-g]) can flaky biscuits

Poppy seeds (optional)

CORNED BEEF HASH WITH FRIED EGG

Corned Beef Hash is a family favorite, and when I realized I could make it in the air fryer it became a quick breakfast staple! Crispy potatoes, tender beef and sweet onions get topped with perfectly fried eggs for an amazing breakfast.

Rinse and dry the potatoes, then chop them into small cubes.

In a large bowl, combine the potatoes and onion. Add the oil, salt, black pepper and paprika and toss everything together.

Transfer the potato and onion mixture to the air fryer. Air-fry the mixture at 350°F (177°C) for 18 to 20 minutes, shaking the basket and stirring the potatoes and onion occasionally.

Meanwhile, cut the corned beef into large chunks.

Top the potatoes with the corned beef and air-fry the hash at 350°F (177°C) for 7 minutes.

Meanwhile, melt the butter in a large skillet over medium-high heat. Carefully crack the eggs into the skillet. Season them with additional salt and black pepper. Fry the eggs to your liking (for this dish, I like them a little runny).

Divide the corned beef hash among four plates and toss the hash together gently so that you don't break up the corned beef too much. Top the hash with the fried eggs.

MAKES: 4 SERVINGS

2 large baking potatoes

½ small onion, diced

1 tbsp (15 ml) oil of choice

1 tsp salt, plus more as needed

½ tsp black pepper, plus more as needed

½ tsp paprika

1 (12-oz [340-g]) can corned beef

1 tbsp (15 g) butter

4 large eggs

SAUSAGE—SWEET POTATO HASH

If you can't tell, I love a good hash! I often make a hash for dinner. There is just something about the mixture of crispy potatoes, sweet onion and savory meat that works wonderfully together. This hash is super simple, but it's full of flavor. Sweet potatoes and onion roast up perfectly in the air fryer while you crumble some flavorful sausage on the stove. They all come together in one hearty, comforting breakfast. I like to use maple or sage breakfast sausage for this, but feel free to use your favorite.

In a large bowl, combine the sweet potatoes and onion. Toss them with the oil, salt, black pepper and paprika.

Place the potato mixture in the air fryer basket. Air-fry the mixture at 400°F (204°C) for 12 to 16 minutes, stirring the mixture and shaking the basket occasionally.

Meanwhile, in a large skillet over medium heat, cook the sausage for 8 to 10 minutes, breaking it apart as it cooks, until it is browned.

When the potatoes are done, transfer them to the skillet with the sausage, stirring gently to combine.

TIP: This hash is also great with a fried egg on top.

MAKES: 4 SERVINGS

2 medium sweet potatoes, peeled and cut into bite-sized cubes

½ small sweet onion, diced

1 tbsp (15 ml) oil of choice

1 tsp salt

½ tsp black pepper

½ tsp paprika

1 lb (454 g) sage or maple breakfast sausage

ON THE SIDE

I love making veggies and side dishes in my air fryer. It frees up my stove and oven for other dishes, and I can cook the food at the same time as my main dish. You can cook way more things in your air fryer than you think! Rice dishes, casseroles and veggies can all be cooked to perfection in the air fryer. I have never loved vegetables more than I do now after making them in the air fryer. They come out crisp and roasted to perfection. My kids eat way more veggies now that we cook them in the air fryer, which is a win in my book.

GENERAL TSO'S CRISPY BRUSSELS SPROUTS

Brussels sprouts used to get a bad rap, but over the past few years people have been coming around to them. Dare I say Brussels sprouts have even become popular lately? I love them any way I can get them, but roasted is my favorite. It is like the air fryer was made to roast Brussels sprouts. This version is one of my family's favorites.

MAKES: 4 SERVINGS

¼ cup (48 g) sugar

¼ cup (60 ml) distilled white vinegar

1½ tbsp (26 g) ketchup

½ tbsp (8 ml) soy sauce

¼ tsp ground ginger

¼ tsp red pepper flakes

1 tbsp minced garlic

4 cups (400 g) fresh Brussels sprouts

Spray oil

Sesame seeds (optional)

Lay a parchment round in the air fryer basket.

In a large bowl, combine the sugar and vinegar and stir until the sugar is dissolved. Add the ketchup, soy sauce, ginger, red pepper flakes and garlic.

Place all the Brussels sprouts in the air fryer basket and spray them with the spray oil. Shake the basket to coat the Brussels sprouts in the spray oil.

Air-fry the Brussels sprouts at 390°F (199°C) for 15 minutes, shaking the basket occasionally. Pull out the air fryer basket, drizzle the General Tso's sauce over the Brussels sprouts and gently toss to coat them in the sauce.

Air-fry the Brussels sprouts at 390°F (199°C) for an additional 3 to 5 minutes.

Sprinkle the Brussels sprouts with the sesame seeds (if using).

ASIAN ORANGE ROASTED BROCCOLI

I was never a big fan of broccoli until I started roasting it. I like to jazz it up sometimes, and this Asian Orange Roasted Broccoli is heavenly. The orange and broccoli go beautifully well together, and the broccoli gets so crispy in the air fryer. This is perfect on the side of chicken or pork chops.

Place a parchment round in the air fryer basket.

In a large bowl, toss the broccoli with the oil. Place the broccoli in the air fryer basket.

Air-fry the broccoli at 400°F (204°C) for 12 minutes, shaking the basket occasionally.

Meanwhile, in a small saucepan over medium-high heat, combine the red pepper flakes, garlic, ginger, granulated sugar, brown sugar, orange juice, vinegar and soy sauce. Bring the mixture to a boil.

In a small bowl, mix together the water and cornstarch. Add the cornstarch mixture to the saucepan and cook the sauce for 3 to 5 minutes, whisking constantly, until it has thickened. Remove the saucepan from the heat.

Pour the sauce over the broccoli. Toss the broccoli to coat it in the sauce and air-fry it at 400°F (204°C) for 3 to 5 minutes.

MAKES: 4 SERVINGS

4 cups (700 g) broccoli florets

1 tbsp (15 ml) oil of choice

1/8 tsp red pepper flakes

1/2 tbsp (5 g) minced garlic

1/8 tsp ground ginger

2 tbsp (24 g) granulated sugar

2 tbsp (18 g) brown sugar

2 tbsp (30 ml) orange juice

2 tbsp (30 ml) distilled white vinegar

1 tbsp (15 ml) soy sauce

1 tbsp (15 ml) cold water

1/2 tbsp (5 g) cornstarch

BACON-RANCH ROASTED CAULIFLOWER

Cauliflower is a great vegetable to cook in the air fryer. It loves to be roasted and crispy. It also is kind of bland, so it's a blank canvas for all sorts of flavors. My kids love this Bacon-Ranch Roasted Cauliflower that's packed with ranch flavor and a little bacon.

In a large bowl, mix together the oil, ranch seasoning, black pepper and garlic salt. Add the cauliflower and stir to coat it in the oil mixture.

Place all the cauliflower in the air fryer and air-fry it at 400°F (204°C) for 15 minutes, shaking the basket frequently and checking the cauliflower for doneness.

Pull out the air fryer basket and sprinkle the bacon over the top of the cauliflower. Air-fry the cauliflower at 400°F (204°C) for 5 minutes.

MAKES:
4 TO 6 SERVINGS

1 tbsp (15 ml) oil of choice

1 tbsp (9 g) ranch seasoning

⅛ tsp black pepper

¼ tsp garlic salt

8 cups (1.8 kg) frozen cauliflower florets

6 slices precooked bacon, coarsely chopped

TACO-SPICED POTATO WEDGES

Taco Tuesday is a favorite in our house. (Finally, a dinner we all agree on!) One thing I can never figure out is what to have alongside our tacos. Taco-Spiced Potato Wedges are the answer! This recipe yields fluffy, crispy potato wedges seasoned with taco spices and topped with melty cheese—perfect for dipping in salsa or sour cream. These are a huge hit with my family, and I love that they take only minutes in the air fryer and come out perfectly crispy every time. Try these the next time you have taco night!

MAKES: 4 SERVINGS

2 medium baking potatoes

1 tbsp (15 ml) oil of choice

1 tbsp (9 g) taco seasoning

½ cup (56 g) shredded Colby Jack cheese

2 tbsp (12 g) coarsely chopped green onion

Salsa, to serve

Sour cream, to serve

Wash and dry the potatoes, then cut each one into eight wedges.

In a medium bowl, mix together the oil and taco seasoning. Add the potato wedges and toss the wedges until they are evenly coated in the oil mixture. Place the wedges in the air fryer basket in a single layer.

Air-fry the wedges at 400°F (204°C) for 15 to 20 minutes. Remove the air fryer basket and sprinkle the wedges with the Colby Jack cheese. Air-fry the wedges at 400°F (204°C) for 30 seconds to melt the cheese.

Remove the wedges from the air fryer basket and sprinkle them with the green onion.

Serve the wedges with salsa or sour cream for dipping.

TIP: Switch out the Colby Jack with pepper Jack for a spicy kick.

LEMON-GARLIC ASPARAGUS

Asparagus is such a great veggie for the air fryer. It takes just minutes in the air fryer, making it great for busy weeknights. I love to flavor mine with a little lemon and garlic and just let the deliciousness of the roasted asparagus shine through.

In a large bowl, mix together the oil, garlic salt, black pepper, minced garlic and half of the lemon juice. Toss the asparagus in the oil mixture.

Lay the asparagus in the air fryer basket and air-fry it at 400°F (204°C) for 12 to 15 minutes, shaking the basket occasionally.

Remove the asparagus from the air fryer basket. Right before serving, drizzle the asparagus with the remaining lemon juice. Garnish the asparagus with the lemon zest.

**MAKES:
2 TO 3 SERVINGS**

1 tbsp (15 ml) oil of choice

¼ tsp garlic salt

¼ tsp coarse black pepper

2 cloves garlic, minced

Juice of 1 small lemon, divided

1 lb (454 g) asparagus, tough ends trimmed

Zest of 1 small lemon, to serve

MAPLE–CHIPOTLE ROASTED SWEET POTATOES

Sweet potatoes make a great side dish with dinner. These sweet potatoes come together in minutes and roast up nicely in your air fryer. The little kick from the chipotle balances out the sweetness from the potatoes and maple syrup.

In a large bowl, mix together the oil, maple syrup and adobo sauce. Add the sweet potatoes and toss to coat them in the oil mixture.

Place all the sweet potatoes in the air fryer basket and air-fry them at 400°F (204°C) for 12 to 15 minutes, shaking the basket and flipping the sweet potatoes two or three times during the cooking time, until they are crispy.

TIP: You can cut back on the chipotle to make this dish milder, or you can add more if you like the heat.

MAKES:
2 TO 3 SERVINGS

2 tbsp (30 ml) oil of choice

2 tbsp (30 ml) pure maple syrup

2 tbsp (30 ml) adobo sauce from chipotles in adobo

2 medium sweet potatoes, peeled and cut into bite-size pieces

PIMENTO CHEESE CORN MUFFINS

There are certain dinners that just need a corn muffin on the side, like chili or any kind of barbecue. I was so happy to discover I could make corn muffins right in my air fryer and in half the time it would take to bake them. I decided to add a little something special to my usual corn muffins by adding pimento cheese. These are amazing.

In a medium bowl, combine the flour, cornmeal, sugar, salt and baking powder.

In a small bowl, whisk together the milk, butter and egg.

Fold the milk mixture into the flour mixture and stir to combine. Stir in the Cheddar cheese and pimentos.

Lightly spray six silicone muffin liners. Fill each liner about three-fourths full of batter and place them in the air fryer basket.

Air-fry the muffins at 350°F (177°C) for 10 minutes. Insert a toothpick into the center of each muffin. If the toothpick does not come out clean, cook the muffins another 3 to 5 minutes.

Let the muffins cool slightly before serving.

MAKES: 6 MUFFINS

½ cup (60 g) all-purpose flour

½ cup (85 g) cornmeal

3 tbsp (36 g) sugar

1 tsp salt

½ tbsp (6 g) baking powder

½ cup (120 ml) milk

3 tbsp (45 g) butter, melted

1 large egg

1 cup (120 g) shredded Cheddar cheese

1½ tbsp (18 g) pimentos, drained

Spray oil

PARMESAN ZUCCHINI CHIPS

These Parmesan Zucchini Chips are a great side dish, but they cook so quickly that I often make them for a quick snack. The thinly sliced zucchini gets its crunchy coating from panko and Parmesan cheese. Warning: These can be addictive!

Spray the air fryer basket with the spray oil.

In a shallow dish, whisk together the egg and milk. In a second shallow dish, mix together the panko bread crumbs, Parmesan cheese, black pepper and Italian seasoning.

Place the zucchini rounds in the egg mixture. Next, coat each round with the panko mixture.

Lay a single layer of zucchini chips in the air fryer basket. Spray the tops with a little spray oil.

Air-fry the zucchini chips at 400°F (204°C) for 5 minutes. Remove the zucchini chips and set them aside. Repeat this process with the remaining zucchini chips.

Let the zucchini chips cool slightly before serving.

TIP: My boys love eating these with a little ranch for dipping!

MAKES:
4 SERVINGS

Spray oil

1 large egg

1 tbsp (15 ml) milk

1 cup (55 g) panko bread crumbs

¼ cup (45 g) grated Parmesan cheese

⅛ tsp black pepper

¼ tsp Italian seasoning

2 small zucchini, thinly sliced into rounds

ROASTED SOUTHWESTERN CORN

Corn is a staple side dish in our house—we eat it a few times a week. As I was looking at ways to switch it up a bit, I learned that you can roast it in the air fryer. I was sold! In this recipe, I add a little southwestern flair to the corn by adding onions, peppers and some spice. It's perfect for taco night.

Place a parchment round in the air fryer basket.

In a large bowl, combine the oil, cumin, salt, black pepper and chili powder and stir to combine. Add the onions, bell peppers, green chilis and corn, tossing to coat the ingredients in the oil mixture.

Add the corn mixture to the air fryer basket. Air-fry the corn at 400°F (204°C) for 12 minutes, shaking the basket halfway through the cooking time.

TIP: You can use 1 cup (175 g) of frozen sliced bell peppers and onions to save time.

MAKES: 4 SERVINGS

1 tbsp (15 ml) oil of choice

½ tsp ground cumin

¼ tsp salt

¼ tsp black pepper

¼ tsp chili powder

½ cup (65 g) thinly sliced onions

½ cup (46 g) thinly sliced red or green bell peppers

1½ tbsp (23 g) canned diced green chilis, drained

2 cups (288 g) frozen corn

SAUSAGE–STUFFED MUSHROOMS

These simple stuffed mushrooms are so easy to make with just four ingredients and 8 minutes in the air fryer. These are perfect on the side of a nice steak or even on their own with just a salad for dinner. They also make a great appetizer.

MAKES: 24 MUSHROOMS

1 lb (454 g) Italian sausage

3 oz (85 g) cream cheese

24 white button mushrooms

¼ cup (45 g) grated Parmesan cheese

Spray oil

In a medium skillet over medium heat, cook the Italian sausage for 8 to 10 minutes, breaking it apart as it cooks, until it is browned. Add the cream cheese and stir it into the sausage until the two are well combined. Remove the skillet from the heat.

Remove the stems from the mushrooms and lightly wipe them with a damp cloth. Fill each mushroom cap with the sausage mixture. Top each mushroom with a sprinkle of the Parmesan cheese.

Place 12 mushrooms in the air fryer basket and spritz the tops with the spray oil. Air-fry the mushrooms at 390°F (199°C) for 8 minutes. Remove the mushrooms from the air fryer and repeat this process with the remaining 12 mushrooms.

Serve the mushrooms warm.

HONEY–GARLIC ROASTED CARROTS

This is another supersimple vegetable recipe that tastes amazing thanks to the roasting capabilities of the air fryer. Baby carrots are always a hit with everyone, and putting a little garlic and honey on them before roasting them makes them magical! This is my favorite way to make carrots. On a busy school night, I can pop these in the air fryer while I'm preparing the rest of dinner.

In a large bowl, whisk together the oil, honey, black pepper, garlic salt and garlic. Add the baby carrots and toss them with the honey mixture until they are all coated.

Put all the carrots in the air fryer basket and air-fry them at 400°F (204°C) for 20 minutes, shaking the basket occasionally.

**MAKES:
4 SERVINGS**

2 tbsp (30 ml) oil of choice

2 tbsp (30 ml) honey

¼ tsp black pepper

¼ tsp garlic salt

3 cloves garlic, minced

4 cups (960 g) baby carrots

BLACK-EYED PEA PATTIES

I grew up eating a lot of black-eyed peas. They have always been on my grandma's Sunday dinner menu. Sometimes I want to switch things up and I make these Black-Eyed Pea Patties. These little patties are full of flavor and a great new twist on black-eyed peas. They're especially good with a little dollop of my Cajun mayo on top.

To make the black-eyed pea patties, heat a small skillet over medium-high heat. Add the bacon and fry it for 8 to 10 minutes, until it is crispy. Transfer the bacon to a paper towel to drain. Set the skillet over medium heat, leaving the grease in the pan.

To the same skillet, add the onion and bell pepper. Cook the onion and bell pepper until the onion is translucent, 5 to 8 minutes. Transfer the onion and bell pepper to a medium bowl.

Add the black-eyed peas, Cajun seasoning, salt and black pepper to the bowl. Mash the ingredients together with a fork until everything is combined and most of the black-eyed peas are smashed. Add the cooked bacon.

Add the flour, ¼ cup (30 g) at a time, until the mixture is cohesive enough to form into four patties.

Spray the air fryer basket with the spray oil. Place the patties in the air fryer basket and spray the tops with the spray oil. Air-fry the patties at 350°F (177°C) for 15 minutes.

To make the Cajun mayo, mix together the mayonnaise, mustard, garlic, Cajun seasoning, black pepper and lemon juice in a small bowl, stirring until the ingredients are well combined.

Serve the patties with a dollop of the Cajun mayo on top.

MAKES: 4 PATTIES

Black-Eyed Pea Patties

6 slices bacon, coarsely chopped

½ small onion, finely chopped

½ small red or green bell pepper, finely chopped

3 cups (420 g) canned black-eyed peas, drained

½ tsp Cajun seasoning

½ tsp salt

⅛ tsp black pepper

½ to 1½ cups (60 to 180 g) all-purpose flour

Spray oil, as needed

Cajun Mayo

½ cup (110 g) mayonnaise

1½ tsp (8 g) Dijon mustard

1 tsp minced garlic

1 tsp Cajun seasoning

Dash of coarse black pepper

½ tsp fresh lemon juice

MAPLE–BACON BRUSSELS SPROUTS

This is my go-to Brussels sprouts recipe. It is super simple but utterly delicious. These are perfect on weeknights alongside roasted chicken, but they are also great with grilled steaks for company. Bacon and Brussels sprouts are a match made in heaven and in the air fryer.

In a medium bowl, whisk together the oil, maple syrup and black pepper. Add the Brussels sprouts and bacon and stir to coat them in the oil mixture.

Place all of the Brussels sprouts in the air fryer basket. Air-fry the Brussels sprouts at 380°F (193°C) for 15 to 20 minutes, shaking the basket frequently.

**MAKES:
4 SERVINGS**

2 tbsp (30 ml) oil of choice

2 tbsp (30 ml) pure maple syrup

¼ tsp black pepper

1 lb (454 g) fresh Brussels sprouts

6 slices bacon, coarsely chopped

GARLIC–PARMESAN SMASHED POTATOES

These potatoes are where it's at! They are baked in the air fryer, then smashed and seasoned, then air-fried again. They are so easy to make but are fancy enough to serve to guests.

Place all of the potatoes in the air fryer basket and spray them with some spray oil. Air-fry the potatoes at 400°F (204°C) for 15 to 20 minutes. Check the potatoes after 15 minutes—a knife should easily be able to pierce the potatoes.

Carefully take the potatoes out of the air fryer and place them on a large baking sheet or tray. Using a coffee cup with a flat bottom or a potato masher, gently smash each potato down into a disk shape.

In a small bowl, combine the butter, garlic, parsley, garlic salt and black pepper. Brush this butter mixture on the potatoes, then flip the potatoes and brush the butter mixture on the other side.

Place a single layer of the smashed potato rounds into the air fryer. (You will have to cook these in batches.) Air-fry the smashed potatoes at 400°F (204°C) for 5 to 7 minutes.

Pull out the air fryer basket and top each potato with a little Parmesan cheese. Air-fry the potatoes at 400°F (204°C) for 2 minutes. Repeat this process with the remaining smashed potatoes.

Serve the smashed potatoes warm.

TIP: You can serve these with a little sour cream.

MAKES: 4 TO 6 SERVINGS

1 lb (454 g) baby yellow potatoes

Spray oil

4 tbsp (60 g) butter, melted

1 clove garlic, minced

1 tsp finely chopped fresh parsley

¼ tsp garlic salt

¼ tsp black pepper

¼ cup (45 g) grated Parmesan cheese

WHITE CHEDDAR FRIED MAC AND CHEESE

Is there anything better than mac and cheese? Yes—when you roll it in bread crumbs and fry it in the air fryer until it's golden and crispy! This White Cheddar Fried Mac and Cheese is the perfect side dish to any dinner.

To make the mac and cheese, line a large baking sheet with parchment paper.

In a medium saucepan over medium heat, melt the butter. Add the flour to the butter, whisking the two into a paste. Add the milk, salt and black pepper. Let the milk come to a bubble and cook it for 2 minutes to allow it to thicken, then add the Cheddar cheese. Stir the sauce with a spoon until all the cheese is melted. Fold in the pasta. Remove the mac and cheese from the heat and allow it to cool until you can handle it safely.

Using a ¼-cup (60-g) measuring cup, scoop out portions of the mac and cheese and place them on the prepared baking sheet. Freeze the mac and cheese for 1 hour.

Meanwhile, make the breading. In a shallow dish, beat together the eggs and milk.

In a second shallow dish, combine the panko bread crumbs, garlic salt and Parmesan cheese. Take a scoop of the frozen mac and cheese, dunk it into the egg mixture and then roll it in the panko mixture. Repeat this process with all the mac and cheese.

Spray the basket of the air fryer with the spray oil. Place half the mac and cheese balls in the basket and spray those with spray oil. Air-fry the mac and cheese at 350°F (177°C) for 15 minutes. Repeat this process with the remaining mac and cheese. Serve the fried mac and cheese warm.

MAKES: 4 SERVINGS

Mac and Cheese
¼ cup (60 g) butter

¼ cup (30 g) all-purpose flour

2 cups (480 ml) milk

¼ tsp salt

¼ tsp black pepper

2 cups (240 g) shredded white Cheddar cheese

8 oz (227 g) short pasta (like shells or macaroni noodles), cooked to al dente and drained

Breading
2 large eggs

¼ cup (60 ml) milk

1½ cups (83 g) panko bread crumbs

½ tsp garlic salt

¼ cup (45 g) grated Parmesan cheese

Spray oil, as needed

TIP: You can use boxed mac and cheese for this recipe. (I won't tell!)

BACON–CHEDDAR HASSELBACK POTATOES

Baked potatoes in the air fryer are magical. You will never have a better baked potato, I promise. They are fluffy on the inside and crisp on the outside—they are perfection.

As much as I love a classic baked potato, sometimes I switch it up and make these Hasselback potatoes. With the savory bacon and the melty Cheddar between slices of potatoes, they are seriously yummy.

Wash and dry each potato. Pierce each potato in the middle with a knife. Rub each potato with the oil and sprinkle the potatoes with the salt.

Place the potatoes in the air fryer basket and air-fry them at 400°F (204°C) for 35 to 40 minutes.

Meanwhile, in a medium skillet over medium-high heat, fry the bacon for 8 to 9 minutes, until it is crispy. Remove the bacon from the heat. Once the bacon has cooled, break the pieces into crumbles.

Slice each potato across the top, making slits in the potato and being careful not to cut all the way through. Brush the butter into the slits of the potatoes. Measure ¼ cup (30 g) Cheddar cheese per potato and stuff the cheese between the slices. Do the same with the bacon.

Return the potatoes to the air fryer and air-fry them at 350°F (177°C) for 2 minutes, until the cheese has melted. Top the potatoes with the sour cream and chives (if using).

MAKES: 4 POTATOES

4 medium baking potatoes

2 tbsp (30 ml) oil of choice

Salt, as needed

8 slices bacon

4 tbsp (60 g) butter, melted

1 cup (120 g) shredded Cheddar cheese

Sour cream (optional)

Coarsely chopped chives (optional)

HONEY BUTTER–ROASTED CORN ON THE COB

This is another one of my favorite easy side dishes. I love that I can keep ears of corn in my freezer, throw them in the air fryer on busy nights and a few minutes later have a fantastic ear of corn on the cob. Roasting ears of corn in the air fryer gives them such a great flavor, and the honey butter just adds to the corn's natural sweetness. This is a crowd-pleaser for sure.

Place a parchment round in the bottom of the air fryer basket. Put the ears of corn in the basket and air-fry them at 350°F (177°C) for 12 minutes, flipping them once halfway through the cooking time.

Meanwhile, in a small microwave-safe bowl, melt the butter and honey together.

After the corn is done, remove the air fryer basket and brush the corn with the honey butter on all sides.

Sprinkle each ear with the salt and place the basket back in the air fryer. Air-fry the corn at 350°F (177°C) for 3 minutes. Garnish with parsley (if using) and serve.

MAKES:
4 SERVINGS

4 small ears corn

4 tsp (20 g) butter

3 tsp (15 ml) honey

½ tsp salt

Finely chopped parsley (optional)

BROCCOLI–CHEDDAR BAKED POTATOES

The perfect side dish that could be a meal in itself, Broccoli-Cheddar Baked Potatoes are a classic. And for good reason—they are delicious! These are nothing new, but the air fryer takes them over the top by making the baked potatoes oh, so crispy.

Wash and dry each potato. Pierce each of the potatoes in the middle with a knife. Rub each potato with the oil and sprinkle it with the salt. Place the potatoes in the air fryer and air-fry them at 400°F (204°C) for 35 to 40 minutes.

Carefully remove the potatoes from the air fryer. Cut a slit halfway down into each potato, and then make a slit across the previous one, making a cross in the potato.

Grasp both ends of the potato and push inward, which will make the potato "pop."

Add 1 tablespoon (15 g) of the butter to the inside of each potato. Season each one with salt and black pepper. Top each potato with ¼ cup (44 g) of the broccoli and ¼ cup (30 g) of the Cheddar cheese.

Place all the potatoes in the air fryer. Air-fry the potatoes at 350°F (177°C) for 2 minutes to melt the cheese.

MAKES: 4 SERVINGS

4 medium baking potatoes

2 tbsp (30 ml) oil of choice

Salt

4 tbsp (60 g) butter

Black pepper

1 cup (175 g) frozen broccoli florets, cooked according to package directions

1 cup (120 g) shredded Cheddar cheese

JALAPEÑO AND ZUCCHINI CORN FRITTERS

I love corn fritters, and I love to add zucchini to dishes whenever I can. We get an abundance of it from our garden, so I try to sneak it into everything. These Jalapeño and Zucchini Corn Fritters are full of corn, fresh zucchini and a little kick from the jalapeño. They come out perfect.

Place a parchment round in the air fryer basket and spritz it with the spray oil.

In a large bowl, toss the zucchini with ½ teaspoon of the salt. Let the zucchini sit for 10 minutes. Wrap the zucchini in a kitchen towel and squeeze out all of the liquid (this will help prevent soggy fritters).

Meanwhile, heat the butter in a medium skillet over medium heat. Add the onion and garlic. Sauté them for about 5 minutes, until the onion is translucent.

In a medium bowl, whisk together the cornmeal, flour, baking soda, remaining ¾ teaspoon of salt and black pepper.

In a small bowl, whisk together the buttermilk and egg.

To the flour mixture, add the egg mixture, onion-garlic mixture, corn and jalapeños. Stir the batter until the ingredients are just combined.

Using a ¼-cup (60-g) scoop or measuring cup, put a scoop of the fritter batter in the air fryer basket. (You will probably be able to fit 3 to 4 scoops in the basket at a time.)

Lightly spray the tops of the fritters with the spray oil. Air-fry the fritters at 360°F (182°C) for 5 to 6 minutes. Repeat this process with the remaining fritters.

MAKES:
6 TO 8 SERVINGS

Spray oil

2 medium zucchini, finely chopped

1¼ tsp (6 g) salt, divided

1 tbsp (15 g) butter

½ small onion, diced

1 clove garlic, minced

½ cup (85 g) yellow cornmeal

½ cup (60 g) all-purpose flour

¼ tsp baking soda

¼ tsp black pepper

¾ cup (180 ml) buttermilk

1 large egg

1½ cups (216 g) fresh or drained canned corn

1 tbsp (11 g) diced canned or fresh jalapeños

PROSCIUTTO ASPARAGUS BUNDLES

Sometimes the best recipes are the simple classics. You can never go wrong with Prosciutto Asparagus Bundles. Each piece of asparagus is wrapped in salty prosciutto, and the combination is superb. This is a classic recipe but cooked in a new way using the air fryer.

Trim off the thick ends of the asparagus and transfer the asparagus spears to a large baking sheet. Drizzle the asparagus spears with the oil and season them with the black pepper, then toss to coat the asparagus. Wrap 1 slice of the prosciutto around each asparagus spear.

Lay 8 asparagus spears in the air fryer in a single layer. Air-fry the asparagus at 350°F (177°C) for 8 minutes. Repeat this process with the remaining 8 asparagus spears.

MAKES:
4 SERVINGS

16 spears asparagus

2 tsp (10 ml) oil of choice

¼ tsp black pepper

16 slices prosciutto

SESAME–GARLIC ROASTED GREEN BEANS

Who would have thought you could turn something as simple as green beans into something so flavorful just by roasting them in the air fryer? I season these with a little Asian flair for a quick and simple side dish my family loves.

In a large bowl, mix together the oil, soy sauce, vinegar, honey, garlic, red pepper flakes and black pepper. Add the green beans and toss to coat them in the sauce.

Put half of the green beans in the air fryer basket and air-fry them at 400°F (204°C) for 12 to 15 minutes, shaking the basket halfway through the cooking time. Repeat this process with the remaining green beans.

Sprinkle the green beans with the sesame seeds.

MAKES:
4 SERVINGS

1 tbsp (15 ml) sesame oil

1 tsp soy sauce

1 tsp rice wine vinegar

2 tsp (10 ml) honey

1 clove garlic, minced

¼ tsp red pepper flakes

¼ tsp black pepper

1½ lbs (680 g) fresh green beans, trimmed

Sesame seeds

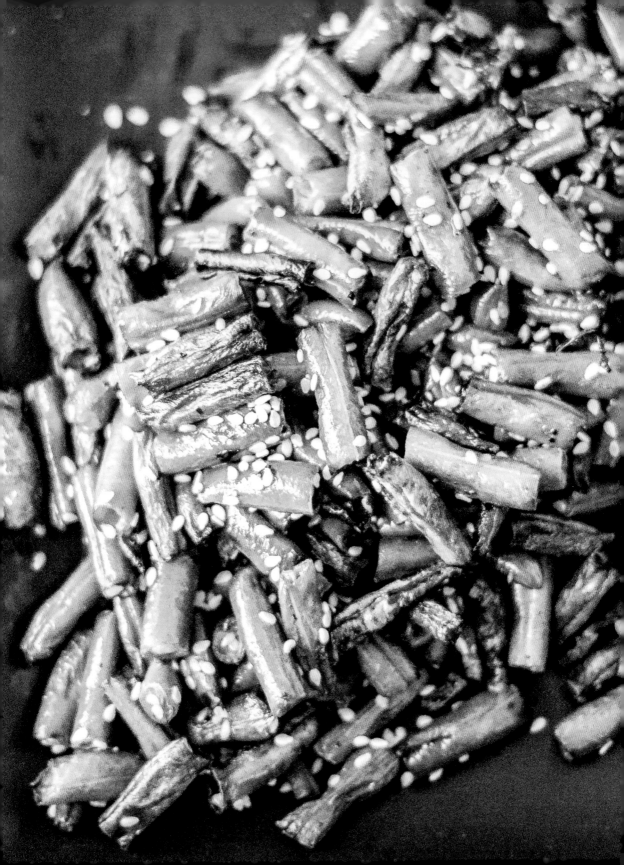

CLASSIC SWEET POTATO CASSEROLE

Sweet potato casserole is usually brought out once a year at Thanksgiving. But why? It is delicious and a great side dish. With your air fryer, you can now make this Classic Sweet Potato Casserole on any weeknight . . . like next Wednesday.

MAKES:
4 SERVINGS

Spray oil

1 (40-oz [1.1-kg]) can cut sweet potatoes, drained

½ cup (72 g) brown sugar

¼ tsp salt

½ tsp ground cinnamon

1 tsp pure vanilla extract

1 large egg, beaten

4 tbsp (60 ml) melted butter

1 cup (50 g) mini marshmallows

½ cup (60 g) pecans

Lightly spray a 1- to 2-quart (960-ml to 1.9-L) baking dish that will fit in your air fryer with the spray oil.

In a large bowl, use a fork to mash the sweet potatoes. Add the brown sugar, salt, cinnamon, vanilla, egg and butter. Stir to combine the ingredients.

Pour the sweet potato mixture into the prepared baking dish. Air-fry the casserole at 350°F (177°C) for 25 to 30 minutes.

Remove the basket from the air fryer and top the casserole with the marshmallows and pecans.

Place the basket back into the air fryer and air-fry the casserole at 350°F (177°C) for 1 to 2 minutes, until the marshmallows are melted and slightly brown.

TIP: Skip the pecans if you like!

CREAMED SPINACH CASSEROLE

What is the best way to prepare spinach? Add some cream and cheese and bake it in the air fryer. This is my favorite way to prepare spinach. This casserole is filled with flavor thanks to onion and garlic. It is great alongside a nice steak.

Spray a 1- to 2-quart (960-ml to 1.9-L) baking dish that fits in your air fryer basket with the spray oil.

In a medium skillet over medium heat, melt the butter. Add the onion and garlic and sauté them for about 5 minutes, until the onion is just becoming translucent.

Add the flour to the onion and garlic, stirring to combine the ingredients. Cook the mixture for 2 to 3 minutes.

Meanwhile, microwave the spinach according to the package directions and place the spinach in a strainer to allow the excess liquid to drain.

Whisk the milk and heavy cream into the onion and garlic mixture. Continue to whisk and bring the mixture to a bubble. Cook it for 5 to 8 minutes to allow it to thicken.

Remove the skillet from the heat.

Add the salt, black pepper and Parmesan cheese, stirring to combine the ingredients. Fold in the spinach.

Pour the spinach mixture into the prepared baking dish and sprinkle the top with additional Parmesan cheese.

Air-fry the casserole at 320°F (160°C) for 8 minutes.

Serve the casserole hot.

MAKES: 4 SERVINGS

Spray oil

4 tbsp (60 g) butter

½ small onion, finely chopped

3 cloves garlic, minced

3 tbsp (24 g) all-purpose flour

12 oz (340 g) frozen spinach

½ cup (120 ml) milk

½ cup (120 ml) heavy cream

¼ tsp salt

¼ tsp black pepper

1 tbsp (11 g) grated Parmesan cheese, plus more as needed

SPINACH–ARTICHOKE CHEESY RICE

Whenever I am struggling to think of a good side dish to go with dinner, my mind often goes to rice. We eat a lot of rice at my house, and sometimes I want to jazz it up and make something a little different. This Spinach-Artichoke Cheesy Rice is inspired by the spinach-artichoke dip everyone craves. I enjoy making this recipe because I can just mix everything together and pop the dish in the air fryer to bake.

Spray a 1- to 2-quart (960-ml to 1.9-L) baking dish that fits your air fryer basket.

In a large bowl, mix together the milk, Parmesan cheese, cream cheese, garlic, salt and black pepper, stirring until the ingredients are well combined. Add the spinach, artichoke hearts and 1 cup (180 g) of the Italian blend cheese. Fold in the rice.

Pour the rice mixture into the prepared baking dish. Air-fry the rice at 350°F (177°C) for 12 to 15 minutes.

Remove the basket from the air fryer and add the remaining ¼ cup (45 g) of Italian blend cheese to the top of the rice. Air-fry the rice at 350°F (177°C) for 1 minute to melt the cheese.

MAKES: 4 SERVINGS

Spray oil

½ cup (120 ml) milk

¼ cup (45 g) grated, shelf-stable Parmesan cheese

6 oz (170 g) cream cheese, softened

2 cloves garlic, minced

½ tsp salt

¼ tsp black pepper

1 cup (180 g) frozen spinach, cooked and drained

1 (14-oz [396-g]) can artichoke hearts, drained and coarsely chopped

1¼ cups (225 g) shredded Italian blend cheese, divided

2 cups (320 g) cooked white rice

THREE-CHEESE GARLIC BREAD

Garlic bread is amazing. Cheesy garlic bread is off the charts. We love any kind of bread in our house, and this Three-Cheese Garlic Bread is one of our favorites to have on spaghetti night. I use half a loaf of French or Italian bread for this recipe, which means we can have it again another night. Yes!

Slice the bread horizontally into 2 slices.

In a small microwave-safe bowl, combine the butter, garlic and garlic salt. Microwave the mixture in 10-second increments until the butter is melted.

Brush the butter onto each slice of the bread. Top each slice of bread with the provolone cheese, mozzarella cheese and Parmesan cheese.

Air-fry 1 slice of bread (or both if you have space in your air fryer) at 350°F (177°C) for 5 minutes.

Garnish the garlic bread with the parsley (if using).

TIP: You can sprinkle some dried oregano on top of the bread for a pop of flavor.

MAKES: 4 TO 6 SERVINGS

½ loaf of French or Italian bread

4 tbsp (60 g) butter

2 cloves garlic, minced

¼ tsp garlic salt

2 to 3 slices provolone cheese

¼ cup (28 g) shredded mozzarella cheese

2 tbsp (22 g) grated Parmesan cheese

Finely chopped fresh parsley, to serve (optional)

SWEET CHILI CAULIFLOWER "WINGS"

These Sweet Chili Cauliflower "Wings" are a quick and healthy alternative when you are craving chicken wings. I simply toss these in my favorite sauce and bread them in a little panko to get all the flavor and crunch I'm craving.

In a large bowl, whisk together the sweet chili sauce and oil. Add the cauliflower and toss to coat it in the sauce.

Place the panko bread crumbs in a medium bowl. Dredge each cauliflower floret in the panko bread crumbs and place it in the air fryer. (You may need to cook this recipe in two batches.)

Lightly spray the cauliflower with the spray oil.

Air-fry the cauliflower at 400°F (204°C) for 15 to 20 minutes, until the "wings" are brown and crispy.

TIP: Try this with your favorite hot sauce in place of the sweet chili sauce.

MAKES: 2 SERVINGS

3 tbsp (45 ml) sweet chili sauce

1 tbsp (15 ml) oil of choice

2 cups (460 g) cauliflower florets

1 cup (55 g) panko bread crumbs

Spray oil

SOUTHERN "FRIED" OKRA

My husband loves fried okra, but I do not love making a mess frying things in my kitchen. So now I make my fried okra in the air fryer and we are both happy. This okra is simple but delicious and gets its flavor from Cajun seasoning and its crispiness from cornmeal.

Spray the air fryer basket with the spray oil.

In a shallow dish, whisk the egg. Add the okra to the egg, tossing to coat the okra. In another shallow dish, mix together the cornmeal, flour and Cajun seasoning.

Place each piece of okra in the cornmeal mixture and flip it to coat it in the cornmeal.

Add half of the okra to the air fryer basket and spritz them with more spray oil.

Air-fry the okra at 400°F (204°C) for 10 minutes, shaking the basket halfway through the cooking time. Repeat this process with the remaining okra.

MAKES:
4 SERVINGS

Spray oil

1 large egg

1 (12-oz [340-g]) bag frozen cut okra

1 cup (170 g) cornmeal

¼ cup (30 g) all-purpose flour

1½ tsp (5 g) Cajun seasoning

CHEESY GARLIC POTATO AU GRATIN

Full of cheese, garlic and potatoes, this dish is sure to wow. It comes together in just minutes but is fancy enough to serve to guests! I really like that it cooks in half the time that it would take me to cook it in the oven.

Butter a 1- to 2-quart (960-ml to 1.9-L) baking dish that fits in the air fryer.

Carefully slice the potatoes into very thin slices.

In a large bowl, mix together the milk, heavy cream, black pepper, garlic salt, garlic and minced onion. Toss the potato slices in the milk mixture.

Scoop half the potatoes into the prepared baking dish. Top the potatoes with half of the white Cheddar cheese, mozzarella cheese and Parmesan cheese. Pour the remaining potatoes into the baking dish and top them with the remaining white Cheddar cheese, mozzarella cheese and Parmesan cheese. Cover the baking dish with foil.

Air-fry the potatoes at 390°F (199°C) for 25 minutes. Let the potatoes au gratin cool slightly before serving.

MAKES: 4 SERVINGS

Butter

3 medium baking potatoes, peeled

¼ cup (60 ml) milk

¼ cup (60 ml) heavy cream

1 tsp black pepper

1 tsp garlic salt

1 tsp minced garlic

1 tsp dried minced onion

½ cup (60 g) shredded white Cheddar cheese

½ cup (56 g) shredded mozzarella cheese

2 tbsp (22 g) grated Parmesan cheese

ROASTED GARLIC AND PARMESAN BROCCOLINI

If you love roasted broccoli, wait until you try this broccolini from the air fryer. I dress this simply with a little garlic and Parmesan, and the flavor is amazing! The air fryer does all the work roasting it to perfection.

In a mixing bowl, toss together the broccolini, oil, garlic salt, black pepper and garlic until the broccolini is well coated.

Place all the broccolini in the air fryer and air-fry it at 375°F (191°C) for 7 to 9 minutes. Sprinkle the broccolini with the Parmesan cheese. Air-fry the broccolini at 375°F (191°C) for 1 to 2 minutes.

TIP: If you can't find broccolini, this recipe is also great with broccoli florets.

MAKES: 4 SERVINGS

1 lb (450 g) broccolini

1 tbsp (15 ml) oil of choice

¼ tsp garlic salt

⅛ tsp black pepper

1 clove garlic, minced

1 tbsp (11 g) grated Parmesan cheese

CHEESE-FILLED GARLIC KNOTS

For this cheesy and easy recipe, I use pizza dough and stuff it full of mozzarella before popping the knots into the air fryer for just 8 minutes—they are done before you could even preheat your oven! We love these alongside dinner, but they also make a great snack.

Place a parchment round in the bottom of the air fryer and spritz it with the spray oil.

In a small microwave-safe bowl, combine the butter, garlic salt and parsley. Microwave the mixture until the butter is melted.

Divide the pizza dough into 16 portions. Cut the mozzarella into 16 pieces.

Flatten out a piece of the pizza dough and place a piece of mozzarella on the dough. Enclose the cheese in the dough and roll it into a ball. Repeat this process with all the cheese and dough.

Place four to six garlic knots in the air fryer and sprinkle a little oregano and Parmesan cheese on each one. Air-fry the garlic knots at 320°F (160°C) for 8 minutes. Repeat this process with the remaining garlic knots.

TIP: Serve the garlic knots with marinara or garlic butter for dipping.

MAKES: 16 KNOTS

Spray oil

3 tbsp (45 g) butter

¼ tsp garlic salt

1 tsp finely chopped fresh parsley

14 to 16 oz (397 to 454 g) pizza dough

1 lb (454 g) fresh mozzarella cheese

1 tsp dried oregano

1 tbsp (11 g) grated Parmesan cheese

SOUTHERN SQUASH

This squash side dish is a no-brainer. It takes just a few minutes of prep and then cooks in your air fryer while you prepare the rest of your meal. This is always a staple in our house, we have it a lot in the summer. A little bacon and sweet onion are all you need to take this squash to the next level.

In a small skillet over medium heat, fry the bacon for 5 to 8 minutes. Once the bacon is crisp, transfer it to paper towels to drain. Do not drain the bacon grease from the skillet.

Add the onion to the skillet with the bacon grease. Cook the onion until it is translucent, about 5 minutes.

Meanwhile, slice the squash into thin rounds. Place the squash in a baking pan that fits in the air fryer basket. Season the squash with the salt and black pepper.

Add the onion and whatever bacon grease was left in the skillet.

Toss the squash with the onions until everything is combined. Place the butter on top of the squash.

Air-fry the squash at 350°F (177°C) for 10 minutes. Stir the squash and air-fry it for another 5 to 8 minutes. Add the bacon and serve.

MAKES:
2 TO 3 SERVINGS

4 slices bacon

½ small onion, diced

2 small yellow squash

1 tsp salt

¼ tsp black pepper

1 tbsp (15 g) butter

POTATO-ONION PANCAKES

These little pancakes are fantastic as a side dish, breakfast, snack—anything, really! We always have the ingredients on hand to make them since they use frozen shredded potatoes and take just about 10 minutes in the air fryer to become perfectly crispy.

Lay a parchment round on the bottom of the air fryer basket and lightly spray it with the spray oil.

In a large bowl, mix together the potatoes, onion, flour, egg, salt and black pepper. Stir until everything is well combined.

Using a ¼-cup (60-g) scoop, transfer some of the potato mixture to the air fryer basket. Flatten each mound out a little with the back of the scoop. (I can fit about 4 scoops in my air fryer, so you will probably need to work in batches.)

Spritz the tops of the pancakes with spray oil and air-fry the pancakes at 350°F (177°C) for 12 minutes. Repeat this process until all the potato mixture is gone.

TIP: We like to eat these with a little sour cream for dipping.

**MAKES:
12 PANCAKES**

Spray oil

2½ cups (525 g) frozen shredded potatoes, thawed

½ cup (100 g) minced onion

3 tbsp (24 g) all-purpose flour

1 large egg, beaten

½ tsp salt

¼ tsp black pepper

SWEET CORN FRITTERS

We eat a lot of corn in my family, and this dish is another variation. These fritters are almost like corncakes but with lots of corn kernels. They're a hit in my family, and I love to serve them alongside our grilled dinners in the summer.

Place a parchment round in the bottom of the air fryer basket and spritz it with the spray oil.

In a large bowl, combine the flour, cornmeal, sugar, salt and baking powder.

In a small bowl, beat together the egg and buttermilk. Add the egg mixture to the flour mixture and stir to combine. Fold in the corn and green onion.

Place 3 to 4 tablespoons (45 to 60 g) of the fritter batter in the air fryer basket to create one fritter. Repeat this process to create a second fritter. Spray the tops with the spray oil.

Air-fry the fritters at 350°F (177°C) for 8 to 10 minutes. Repeat this process with the remaining fritter batter.

MAKES: 8 FRITTERS

Spray oil

¾ cup (90 g) all-purpose flour

1 tbsp (11 g) cornmeal

½ tbsp (6 g) sugar

½ tsp salt

1 tsp baking powder

1 large egg

¼ cup (60 ml) buttermilk

1 cup (144 g) fresh, canned or frozen corn (drained if canned, thawed if frozen)

1 tbsp (6 g) coarsely chopped green onion

ALMOND RICE

This Almond Rice is a quick side dish for any main dish you are having. It goes great with chicken, steak, pork, seafood—anything you are serving. It comes together in no time and even your pickiest eaters will ask for seconds. I love the taste of toasted almonds, and they are the highlight of this recipe.

Use a little butter to grease a 1- to 2-quart (960-ml to 1.9-L) baking dish that fits in the air fryer basket.

In a small microwave-safe bowl, combine the butter, garlic and green onions. Microwave the mixture until the butter is melted.

In a medium bowl, mix together the rice, garlic butter, salt, black pepper and ¼ cup (28 g) of the almonds.

Pour the rice mixture into the prepared baking dish and top it with the remaining ¼ cup (27 g) of almonds.

Air-fry the Almond Rice at 350°F (177°C) for 10 minutes.

TIP: You can use sliced or slivered almonds. You could also try pecans instead of almonds.

MAKES: 4 SERVINGS

3 tbsp (45 g) butter, plus more as needed

2 cloves garlic, minced

2 green onions, coarsely chopped

2 cups (320 g) cooked white rice

1 tsp salt

½ tsp black pepper

½ cup (55 g) slivered almonds, divided

GREEN BEAN CASSEROLE

This is another dish that only seems to come out during the holidays, though I love to eat it year-round. This is the classic recipe we all love, but it's made in half the time of the traditional way. You can have your beloved holiday classic any night of the week!

In a large bowl, combine the mushroom soup, milk, soy sauce and black pepper. Add the green beans and ⅔ cup (37 g) of the French fried onions.

Pour the green bean mixture into a 1½-quart (1.4-L) baking dish that fits in the air fryer basket.

Air-fry the casserole at 350°F (177°C) for 10 minutes. Top the casserole with the Cheddar cheese (if using) and the remaining ⅔ cup (36 g) of French fried onions. Air-fry the casserole at 350°F (177°C) for another 2 minutes.

Serve the casserole warm.

MAKES:
6 SERVINGS

1 (11-oz [312-g]) can cream of mushroom soup

½ cup (120 ml) milk

1 tsp soy sauce

⅛ tsp black pepper

4 cups (720 g) drained canned green beans

1⅓ cups (73 g) French fried onions, divided

½ cup (60 g) shredded Cheddar cheese (optional)

PIMENTO CHEESE RICE CASSEROLE

Being southern, my family loves our pimento cheese. I try to put it on and in everything I can. This rice is so good with the addition of the cheese and pimentos. It is a great side dish that can go with any meal. We love it alongside tacos—yum!

Use a little butter to grease a 1- to 2-quart (960-ml to 1.9-L) baking dish that fits in the air fryer basket.

In a large bowl, mix together the butter, milk, pimentos, 1 cup (120 g) of the Cheddar cheese, salt, black pepper and green onion. Fold in the rice until everything is combined.

Pour the rice mixture into the prepared baking dish and top the casserole with the remaining ½ cup (60 g) of Cheddar cheese.

Air-fry the casserole at 350°F (177°C) for 10 minutes.

Serve the casserole warm.

TIP: Use half Cheddar cheese and half pepper Jack cheese for a bit of heat!

MAKES:
4 SERVINGS

3 tbsp (45 g) butter, softened, plus more as needed

½ cup (120 ml) milk

4 oz (113 g) chopped pimentos, drained

1½ cups (180 g) shredded Cheddar cheese, divided

¼ tsp salt

⅛ tsp black pepper

1 tbsp (6 g) coarsely chopped green onion

2 cups (320 g) cooked white rice

BROCCOLI-CHEDDAR TOTS

Do you have a hard time getting your kids to eat their veggies? Sometimes I have a hard time even getting my husband to eat his veggies! I know that we all can get a little tired of the same old veggies. That's why these Broccoli-Cheddar Tots are such a good way to entice your picky eaters to eat more veggies: These tots are full of broccoli and cheese and are flavored with some garlic to make them extra tasty.

Place a parchment round in the air fryer basket and spritz it with the spray oil.

Cut the broccoli into chunks and transfer them to the food processor. Add ¼ teaspoon of the salt and process the broccoli a few times until it is finely chopped. Wrap the broccoli in a clean kitchen towel and twist the top, squeezing some of the moisture out of the broccoli. Place the broccoli, still in the towel, in a strainer and let it drain for about 2 minutes. Give it another big squeeze to get more liquid out. Let the broccoli sit for 20 minutes, until the salt has drawn out any remaining moisture.

In a large bowl, combine the broccoli, bread crumbs, green onion, Cheddar cheese, garlic, remaining ¼ teaspoon of salt, black pepper and egg. Mix the ingredients together until they are well combined.

Form the mixture into 14 to 16 tots. Place the tots in the air fryer and air-fry them at 380°F (193°C) for 10 minutes.

MAKES:
3 TO 4 SERVINGS

Spray oil, as needed

1 large head broccoli

½ tsp salt, divided

⅓ cup (40 g) traditional bread crumbs

2 tbsp (12 g) coarsely chopped green onion

⅔ cup (80 g) shredded Cheddar cheese

1 clove garlic, minced

¼ tsp black pepper

1 large egg

CHEESY RICE BALLS

Since we eat so much rice in our family, we often have it left over. What is my favorite thing to do with it? Mix it with some cheese and throw it in the air fryer. This makes a delicious side dish or even a snack. My kids love these—everybody does! I like that they take just minutes in the air fryer and come out crispy and ooey-gooey cheesy.

Place a parchment round in the bottom of the air fryer basket and spritz it with the spray oil.

In a large bowl, combine the rice, garlic salt, black pepper and Italian blend cheese.

Place the flour in a shallow dish. Place the eggs in a second shallow dish. In a third shallow dish, mix together the bread crumbs and Parmesan cheese.

Scoop about 1½ tablespoons (23 g) of the rice mixture into your hand and shape into a ball.

Coat the rice ball in the flour, then the egg, then roll it in the bread crumb mixture.

Place half of the rice balls in the air fryer and spray the tops with spray oil.

Air-fry the rice balls at 400°F (204°C) for 10 minutes. Repeat this process with the rest of the rice mixture.

TIP: Serve these rice balls with warm marinara for dipping.

**MAKES:
4 SERVINGS**

Spray oil

2 cups (320 g) cooked white rice

¼ tsp garlic salt

¼ tsp black pepper

1 cup (180 g) shredded Italian blend cheese

1 cup (120 g) all-purpose flour

2 large eggs, beaten

2 cups (240 g) Italian-seasoned bread crumbs

¼ cup (45 g) grated Parmesan cheese

BAKED THREE-CHEESE MAC AND CHEESE

If you have picky eaters like I do, you know macaroni and cheese is a lifesaver. I swear, some days it is all my youngest will eat. That's okay, because I can make this fabulous Baked Three-Cheese Mac and Cheese right in my air fryer. This recipe is luscious, creamy and cheesy—everything my kids and I love in a mac and cheese. You can make this in one dish, but I like to divide it among little ramekins for individual servings.

In a medium saucepan over medium heat, melt 3 table-spoons (45 g) of the butter. Whisk in the flour, salt and black pepper. Increase the heat to medium-high. Add the milk, whisking to combine the ingredients, and cook the mixture for 5 to 8 minutes, until it is thick.

Stir in the Cheddar cheese, cream cheese and 2 tablespoons (22 g) of the Parmesan cheese. Cook the sauce for 3 to 5 minutes, until the cheeses are melted.

Remove the saucepan from the heat. Fold the pasta into the sauce.

Divide the mac and cheese among four to six ramekins.

In a small microwave-safe bowl, microwave the remaining 1 tablespoon (15 g) of butter until it is melted. Add the bread crumbs, the remaining 2 tablespoons (22 g) of Parmesan cheese and parsley. Evenly divide the breadcrumb mixture over the top of each ramekin of mac and cheese.

Air-fry the mac and cheese at 350°F (177°C) for 7 minutes.

Let the mac and cheese cool slightly before serving.

MAKES:
4 TO 6 SERVINGS

4 tbsp (60 g) butter, divided

¼ cup (30 g) all-purpose flour

1 tsp salt

¼ tsp black pepper

2 cups (480 ml) milk

2 cups (240 g) shredded Cheddar cheese

4 oz (113 g) cream cheese

4 tbsp (44 g) Parmesan cheese, divided

8 oz (227 g) short pasta (like macaroni or shells), cooked to al dente

¼ cup (30 g) traditional bread crumbs

½ tbsp (2 g) finely chopped fresh parsley

QUICK AND EASY MAIN DISHES

We already know that the air fryer is fantastic at making food super crispy and crunchy without using all that oil. But the other draw of an air fryer is how fast it cooks things! Its speed makes it perfect for main dishes. I am a busy mom and there are nights I just need a quick and easy dinner without picking up the phone for takeout or hitting a drive-through. All the recipes in this chapter come together quickly and are easy to put together. They save my life on those busy nights when everyone is asking what's for dinner and I'm short on time. These recipes are also fabulous quick lunches—so really, they're perfect for anytime!

PESTO CHICKEN MINI PIZZAS

I think we all grew up eating those easy English muffin pizzas. They were delicious then, and they still are! But I gave them an upgrade by adding some chicken and flavorful pesto. I use leftover or rotisserie chicken for this recipe, and all the flavor comes from the pesto. These come together in minutes and make a fast dinner with a salad on the side.

In a medium bowl, toss the chicken with the pesto. Place one-eighth of the chicken on each English muffin half. Top each English muffin with ¼ cup (28 g) of the mozzarella cheese.

Put four pizzas at a time in the air fryer and air-fry them at 350°F (177°C) for 5 minutes. Repeat this process with the other four pizzas.

**MAKES:
4 SERVINGS**

2 cups (250 g) shredded cooked chicken

¾ cup (188 g) pesto

4 English muffins, split

2 cups (224 g) shredded mozzarella cheese

TURKEY CLUB SLIDERS

These little Turkey Club Sliders are a favorite with my kids and a favorite of mine because I can whip them up in minutes. I heat them up in the air fryer until the cheese is melty. Topped with a little butter and some poppy and sesame seeds, these are one quick lunch or dinner option that makes everyone happy!

Place a parchment round in the air fryer basket.

Separate all the rolls and slice them in half. Cut each slice of Cheddar cheese into quarters. Place one piece of cheese on the bottom half of each roll. Divide the turkey among all the rolls.

Break each slice of bacon in half and place two halves on each roll. Top each roll with the remaining cheese quarters. Top each slider with the top bun.

Place six rolls in the air fryer basket.

In a small bowl, mix together the butter, mustard, garlic salt, onion powder and Worcestershire sauce. Brush the top of each slider with the sauce and sprinkle each with the poppy seeds and sesame seeds.

Air-fry the sliders at 350°F (177°C) for 5 to 7 minutes, until the cheese has melted. Repeat this process with the remaining sliders.

MAKES: 12 SLIDERS

12 Hawaiian rolls

6 slices Cheddar cheese

1 lb (454 g) shaved or thinly sliced deli turkey

12 slices cooked bacon

2 tbsp (30 ml) melted butter

1 tbsp (15 g) Dijon mustard

½ tsp garlic salt

½ tsp onion powder

1 tsp Worcestershire sauce

1 tbsp (8 g) poppy seeds

1 tbsp (10 g) sesame seeds

ENGLISH MUFFIN TUNA MELT

This is a classic lunch item you can't go wrong with. The tuna melt is a fabulous combination that I love to serve on an English muffin. This is such a fast lunch, and the air fryer toasts the English muffins superbly and gets that cheese perfectly melty.

In a medium bowl, combine the tuna, egg, celery, onion, mayonnaise, mustard and black pepper. Mix all the ingredients together, making sure to mash the egg.

Spread the tuna salad evenly among all the English muffin halves.

Top each sandwich with a slice of the Cheddar cheese.

Place four sandwiches in the air fryer at a time. Air-fry the sandwiches at 370°F (188°C) for 5 to 7 minutes, just until the cheese has melted. Repeat this process with the remaining sandwiches.

Sprinkle the tuna melt with the parsley (if using).

MAKES:
4 SERVINGS

2 (5-oz [142-g]) cans tuna packed in water, drained

1 large hard-boiled egg, peeled

1½ tbsp (9 g) minced celery

1½ tbsp (20 g) minced red onion

⅓ cup (73 g) mayonnaise

1 tbsp (15 g) Dijon mustard

¼ tsp black pepper

4 English muffins, split

8 slices Cheddar cheese

Finely chopped fresh parsley, to serve (optional)

SPINACH-ALFREDO FRENCH BREAD PIZZA

French bread pizza: Who hasn't lived off of that for a while? This is another quick recipe I pull out when the evening is getting late and everyone is hungry or on those days when I've got a house full of people and everyone wants lunch. I put a little twist on it by topping this with fresh spinach and creamy Alfredo sauce.

Cut the bread in half horizontally.

Spread roughly ¼ cup (60 ml) of the Alfredo sauce on each half of the bread. Spread 1 cup (180 g) of the Italian blend cheese all over the top of each half. Arrange ½ cup (15 g) of the baby spinach on each half. Sprinkle 1 tablespoon (11 g) of the Parmesan cheese on each half.

Put one half of the bread in the air fryer and air-fry it at 390°F (199°C) for 7 minutes. Repeat this process with the other half of the bread.

Let the bread cool slightly and slice it into pieces.

MAKES: 4 SERVINGS

½ loaf French or Italian bread

½ cup (120 ml) Alfredo sauce

2 cups (360 g) shredded Italian blend cheese

1 cup (30 g) baby spinach

2 tbsp (22 g) grated Parmesan cheese

HONEY MUSTARD CHICKEN AND POTATO FOIL PACKETS

Foil packet dinners were made for the air fryer, they just didn't know it. Tender chicken and baby potatoes get cooked together in a luscious honey mustard sauce right in the air fryer. Everyone gets their own little packet, and everyone is happy.

Wash and dry the potatoes. Cut them in halves or quarters, depending on how large they are.

In a large bowl, whisk together the honey, mustard, garlic salt and black pepper.

On a work surface, arrange four (8- to 12-inch [20- to 30-cm]) pieces of heavy-duty foil. Place a chicken breast on each piece of foil. Arrange the onion and potatoes around the chicken. Top each portion with one quarter of the sauce. Fold together the long sides of the foil, and then fold and roll up the short ends of the foil to create a packet.

Place the packets in the air fryer and air-fry them at 400°F (204°C) for 25 to 30 minutes, until the potatoes are tender.

MAKES:
4 SERVINGS

1 lb (454 g) baby potatoes

⅓ cup (80 ml) honey

2 tbsp (30 g) Dijon mustard

¼ tsp garlic salt

¼ tsp black pepper

4 (4-oz [113-g]) boneless, skinless chicken breasts

½ small red onion, thinly sliced

BACON EGG SALAD

Egg salad from the air fryer? Well, kind of! You can make hard-boiled eggs in the air fryer and you can make bacon in the air fryer—combine the two and you have one superdelicious Bacon Egg Salad.

Place the eggs in the air fryer and air-fry them at 250°F (121°C) for 17 minutes. Remove the eggs from the air fryer and place them in an ice bath to cool off.

Place all of the bacon in the air fryer. Air-fry the bacon at 400°F (121°C) for 10 minutes, checking halfway through the cooking time to see if it will need less time.

Remove the bacon from the air fryer when it is crisp, and transfer it to paper towels to cool.

In a medium bowl, combine the mayonnaise, mustard, Worcestershire sauce, sugar, black pepper and hot sauce.

Next, peel your eggs and add them to the bowl. Mash the eggs with a fork into the sauce. You want to leave the eggs a little chunky. Next crumble in your bacon and stir to combine.

Divide the egg salad among the croissants.

MAKES: 4 SERVINGS

6 large eggs

6 slices bacon

¼ cup (55 g) mayonnaise

1 tbsp (15 g) yellow mustard

1½ tsp (8 ml) Worcestershire sauce

¼ tsp sugar

¼ tsp black pepper

Dash of hot sauce

4 croissants, sliced in half

SOUTHWESTERN TILAPIA

I love a good piece of crispy tilapia, but I hate frying anything. So I air-fry my fish and it comes out perfect every time. I am a huge fan of cornmeal breading on my fish, and that works so well in the air fryer. This Southwestern Tilapia is perfectly spiced, and I love to serve it with Roasted Southwestern Corn (page 168).

Spray the bottom of the air fryer basket with the spray oil.

In a shallow dish, mix together the cornmeal, chili powder, onion powder, red pepper flakes, oregano, paprika, cumin and garlic salt.

Place the water in another shallow dish.

Dip each piece of tilapia in the water, and then coat it in the cornmeal mixture.

Place 4 tilapia fillets in the air fryer basket and spray them generously with the spray oil.

Air-fry the tilapia fillets at 400°F (204°C) for 8 minutes, flipping them once halfway through the cooking time. Repeat this process with the remaining tilapia.

TIP: This crispy fish is great on top of salads, in wraps and just as is!

MAKES:
4 SERVINGS

Spray oil

2 cups (340 g) cornmeal

1 tbsp (9 g) chili powder

¼ tsp onion powder

¼ tsp red pepper flakes

¼ tsp dried oregano

½ tsp paprika

1½ tsp (5 g) ground cumin

1 tsp garlic salt

1 cup (240 ml) water

8 (4-oz [113-g]) tilapia fillets

BEEF AND BEAN ENCHILADAS

This is one dinner my family asks me for weekly. Beef and Bean Enchiladas are simple and satisfying. The tortillas are stuffed with refried beans and two kinds of cheese before being topped with ground beef and red sauce—oh, and more cheese! I cook these in the air fryer in half the time of traditional enchiladas, which means I can make them more often for my family.

MAKES: 4 SERVINGS

Spray two square baking dishes that fit in the air fryer with the spray oil.

In a medium skillet over medium heat, cook the beef for 8 to 10 minutes, breaking it apart as it cooks, until it is browned. Drain off any grease.

Add the enchilada sauce to the beef and remove the skillet from the heat.

Lay out the tortillas on a work surface and evenly distribute the refried beans among the tortillas, spreading the beans out across each tortilla.

Divide 1 cup (120 g) of the Cheddar cheese among the tortillas. Divide 1 cup (112 g) of the pepper Jack cheese among the tortillas.

Roll up the tortillas and place 4 in each of the prepared baking dishes. Pour half of the meat mixture over each batch of enchiladas. Divide the remaining ½ cup (60 g) of Cheddar cheese and the remaining ½ cup (56 g) of pepper Jack cheese between the batches of enchiladas.

Place one baking dish at a time in the air fryer. Air-fry the enchiladas at 350°F (177°C) for 7 to 10 minutes. Repeat this process with the remaining enchiladas.

Serve the enchiladas topped with the sour cream and green onion.

Ingredients

Spray oil

1 lb (454 g) ground beef

1 (28-oz [828-ml]) can red enchilada sauce

8 (8-inch [20-cm]) flour tortillas

1 (15-oz [425-g]) can refried beans

1½ cups (180 g) shredded Cheddar cheese, divided

1½ cups (168 g) shredded pepper Jack cheese, divided

Sour cream, to serve

Coarsely chopped green onion, to serve

TIP: Skip the ground beef in the sauce to make this a great meatless option.

HONEY-GARLIC VEGGIE SKEWERS

These Honey-Garlic Veggie Skewers are packed full of flavor and veggies. They are a quick meal with no meat, great for those Meatless Mondays. I love to serve these over steamed rice.

In a large bowl, mix together the oil, brown sugar, soy sauce, honey, garlic, garlic salt and black pepper. Add the onion, green bell pepper, red bell pepper, zucchini, yellow squash and mushrooms to the sauce and let them marinate for 15 minutes.

Skewer all of the veggies on metal skewers. Place the skewers in the air fryer. Air-fry the skewers at 380°F (193°C) for 10 minutes, flipping them halfway through the cooking time.

MAKES:
4 SERVINGS

1 tbsp (15 ml) oil of choice

¾ cup (108 g) brown sugar

3 tbsp (45 ml) soy sauce

1 tbsp (15 ml) honey

2 cloves garlic, minced

½ tsp garlic salt

¼ tsp black pepper

1 small red onion, quartered

1 medium green bell pepper, cut into bite-sized pieces

1 medium red bell pepper, cut into bite-sized pieces

1 medium zucchini, thickly sliced

1 medium yellow squash, thickly sliced

1 lb (454 g) white button mushrooms, stems removed

BLACKENED CHICKEN TENDERLOINS

Some nights I just want an easy dinner that is simple to make. These Blackened Chicken Tenderloins are packed with flavor, and I love that I can make them in minutes in the air fryer. But my favorite part of this recipe is that these tenderloins go with anything: You can serve them with salad or potatoes, you can top pasta with them, you can pop them in a tortilla. There are so many things you can do with these, but they are also awesome just on their own.

Spray the air fryer basket with the spray oil.

In a small bowl, mix together the paprika, garlic salt, cayenne pepper, cumin, thyme, black pepper and onion powder. Rub each chicken tenderloin with the seasoning until it is well coated.

Place the chicken in the air fryer basket. Spray the chicken with the spray oil.

Air-fry the chicken at 360°F (182°C) for 8 to 10 minutes, until the chicken's internal temperature reaches 165°F (74°C).

MAKES: 4 SERVINGS

Spray oil

1 tsp paprika

¼ tsp garlic salt

¼ tsp cayenne pepper

½ tsp ground cumin

½ tsp dried thyme

¼ tsp black pepper

¼ tsp onion powder

8 boneless, skinless chicken tenderloins

THREE-INGREDIENT PORK CHOPS

Just three ingredients are all you need to make the best pork chops. Make sure to serve some rice on the side, because you will definitely want it to soak up the sauce—yum!

Place 4 pork chops in each of two square baking dishes that fit in the air fryer.

In a small bowl, mix together the brown sugar and Italian dressing mix. Spoon half of the seasoning mixture over the pork chops in each baking dish. Pat the brown sugar mixture onto each pork chop. Let some of the mixture fall to the bottom of the baking dishes as well, because that will create the sauce.

Place one baking dish in the air fryer. Air-fry the pork chops at 400°F (204°C) for 9 minutes. Repeat the process with the remaining pork chops.

TIP: The sauce should be sticky and perfect for spooning over rice.

MAKES: 4 TO 6 SERVINGS

8 (4-oz [113-g]) boneless pork chops

1 cup (144 g) brown sugar

2 (1-oz [28-g]) packets dry zesty Italian dressing mix

TURKEY–BACON–RANCH CROISSANTS IN FOIL

Turkey-Bacon-Ranch Croissants in Foil are a staple in my house. I like to make a bunch at the beginning of the week, and whenever we need a quick dinner or a fast lunch, we just pop one in the air fryer and warm it up a bit—in minutes, we have a warm, cheesy, filling sandwich.

Spread each half of the croissants with ½ tablespoon (8 ml) of the ranch dressing. Place 1 slice of the Cheddar cheese on the bottom half of each croissant. Evenly divide the turkey among the four sandwiches. Top each sandwich with 2 slices of bacon. Add another slice of Cheddar cheese on top. Top each sandwich with the top half of the croissant.

Wrap each sandwich in foil. Place the sandwiches in the air fryer and air-fry them at 350°F (177°C) for 8 minutes.

Serve the sandwiches warm.

MAKES: 4 SERVINGS

4 croissants, sliced in half

4 tbsp (60 ml) ranch dressing

8 slices Cheddar cheese

8 oz (227 g) smoked deli turkey

8 slices cooked bacon

CHICKEN TERIYAKI SKEWERS

When I order Chinese takeout, I always get an order of the chicken teriyaki skewers—they are my favorite! Now I can make them at home in no time in my air fryer. They come out with crispy ends, just like the delivery option. But you can make yours faster than you could get them delivered, and that's a win in my book.

In a small bowl, mix together the soy sauce, pineapple juice, garlic, ginger, brown sugar and sesame seeds until the ingredients are well combined.

In a gallon (3.8-L) ziplock bag, combine the chicken and teriyaki sauce. Allow the chicken to marinate for 1 hour.

Skewer the chicken onto metal skewers. Place as many skewers as will fit in a single layer in the air fryer. Air-fry the skewers at 380°F (193°C) for 8 to 10 minutes, until the chicken's internal temperature reaches 165°F (74°C). Repeat the process with the remaining skewers, if needed.

Serve the chicken skewers over the rice.

MAKES:
4 TO 6 SERVINGS

1 cup (240 ml) low-sodium soy sauce

½ cup (120 ml) pineapple juice

2 cloves garlic, minced

¼ tsp ground ginger

¾ cup (108 g) brown sugar

1 tbsp (10 g) sesame seeds

2 lbs (900 g) boneless, skinless chicken thighs, cut into bite-sized pieces

Cooked white or fried rice, to serve

BARBECUE CHICKEN POCKETS

A crowd-pleaser and time-saver, these Barbecue Chicken Pockets are simple to make and full of barbecue chicken and Cheddar cheese. I like to serve these with a side of mac and cheese and some deviled eggs: the perfect quick dinner everyone will love.

Place a parchment round in the bottom of the air fryer and spritz it with the spray oil.

Gently roll the pizza dough into a rectangle. Cut the dough into four smaller, even rectangles.

In a medium bowl, mix together the chicken, barbecue sauce, Colby Jack cheese and onion. Scoop a quarter of the chicken mixture onto each dough rectangle.

Fold the dough in half over the filling, then crimp the edges with a fork.

Place two chicken pockets in the air fryer and spritz the tops with the spray oil. Air-fry the chicken pockets at 360°F (182°C) for 10 minutes. Repeat this process with the remaining chicken pockets.

MAKES: 4 SERVINGS

Spray oil

14 to 16 oz (397 to 454 g) refrigerated pizza dough

2 cups (250 g) shredded cooked chicken

¼ cup (60 ml) barbecue sauce

2 cups (224 g) shredded Colby Jack cheese

½ small red onion, thinly sliced

SPICY CHICKEN CAESAR SALAD

This Spicy Chicken Caesar Salad is one of my favorite lunches, but it also makes a great dinner. I make this a lot in the summer when it is just too hot to eat anything warm. I make the croutons and spicy chicken strips in my air fryer, which means I don't have to heat up the kitchen with the oven.

To make the salad, spray the basket of the air fryer with the spray oil.

In a small bowl, mix together the garlic salt, onion powder, black pepper, cayenne pepper and paprika. Rub the mixture on the chicken tenderloins.

Place the chicken tenderloins in the air fryer basket and spray them with the spray oil.

Air-fry the chicken at 360°F (182°C) for 8 to 10 minutes, until the chicken's internal temperature reaches 165°F (74°C).

To make the croutons, cut the bread into bite-sized cubes. In a large bowl, combine the oil, garlic salt and Parmesan cheese. Add the bread cubes and toss to coat them in the oil mixture. Place the bread cubes in the air fryer and air-fry them at 400°F (204°C) for 5 minutes. Let the croutons cool.

Meanwhile, in a large bowl, toss the lettuce with the Caesar dressing. Top the salad with the chicken. Sprinkle some shaved Parmesan cheese over the top of the salad, then add the croutons.

MAKES: 2 TO 4 SERVINGS

Salad
Spray oil

½ tbsp (5 g) garlic salt

¼ tsp onion powder

¼ tsp black pepper

½ tsp cayenne pepper

1 tsp paprika

1 lb (450 g) boneless, skinless chicken tenderloins

1 large head romaine lettuce, coarsely chopped

1 cup (240 ml) Caesar dressing

Shaved Parmesan cheese, to serve

Croutons
3 thick slices bread

2 tbsp (30 ml) olive oil

½ tsp garlic salt

1 tbsp (11 g) grated Parmesan cheese

SAUSAGE-AND-PEPPERS PIGS IN A BLANKET

Sausage and peppers make a great sub, but they make even better pigs in a blanket. I use Italian sausage and sautéed peppers and onions and roll them all up in a flaky crescent roll dough. They are a hit every time!

Spritz the air fryer basket with the spray oil.

Melt the butter in a medium skillet over medium heat. Add the green bell pepper, red bell pepper and onion and cook for 5 to 8 minutes, until they have softened and are just starting to caramelize. Remove the vegetables from the skillet and set them aside.

Unroll the crescent roll dough and pinch two of the crescents together at the seam to create a rectangle. Repeat this process to create seven more rectangles. Place an Italian sausage on each rectangle and spoon some of the peppers and onions over the top of the sausage.

Roll the sausages up in the dough, sealing the dough at the seam and tucking the ends under.

Place four pigs in a blanket in the air fryer basket. Air-fry them at 390°F (199°C) for 8 minutes. Repeat this process with the remaining pigs in a blanket.

MAKES:
8 PIGS IN A BLANKET

Spray oil

2 tbsp (30 g) butter

½ small green bell pepper, thinly sliced

½ small red bell pepper, thinly sliced

½ small onion, thinly sliced

2 (8-oz [227-g]) cans crescent rolls

8 precooked Italian sausages

GARLICKY STEAK AND POTATOES

You can't go wrong with meat and potatoes, right? This recipe for Garlicky Steak and Potatoes is just that. Fabulously seasoned steak and tender roasted potatoes cook together in your air fryer and come out perfect every time. This dinner is seriously fast and seriously delicious.

To make the potatoes, combine the oil, garlic salt, paprika, black pepper and garlic. Add the potatoes and toss them in the oil mixture to coat.

Put all the potatoes in the air fryer and air-fry them at 400°F (204°C) for 12 minutes, shaking the basket halfway through the cooking time.

To make the steak, combine the steak seasoning, black pepper, garlic salt and garlic in a large bowl. Add the steak and toss to coat the steak with the seasoning.

Put the steak in the air fryer with the potatoes and air-fry the mixture at 400°F (204°C) for 6 to 8 minutes, shaking the basket halfway through the cooking time. If the steak is not cooked to your liking, cook it for 1 more minute.

MAKES: 2 SERVINGS

Potatoes

1 tbsp (15 ml) oil of choice

½ tsp garlic salt

½ tsp paprika

¼ tsp black pepper

2 cloves garlic, minced

8 oz (227 g) baby potatoes, halved

Steak

2 tsp (6 g) steak seasoning (I like Montreal)

¼ tsp black pepper

¼ tsp garlic salt

2 cloves garlic, minced

2 (4-oz [113-g]) boneless steaks of choice, cut into bite-sized pieces

FAJITA-STUFFED CHICKEN

This Fajita-Stuffed Chicken is full of bell peppers, onions and cheese and seasoned with fajita spices. Everything cooks in the air fryer and is great over a bed of rice and beans. So easy, quick and delicious!

**MAKES:
4 SERVINGS**

Spray the air fryer basket with the spray oil.

Melt the butter in a medium skillet over medium heat. Add the green bell pepper, red bell pepper and onion and cook them for 10 to 15 minutes, until they are caramelized. Remove the vegetables from the skillet and set them aside to cool.

Meanwhile, cut a deep pocket in the side of each chicken breast.

In a small bowl, mix together the chili powder, garlic salt, paprika, sugar, onion powder, cayenne pepper, black pepper and cumin.

Stuff each chicken breast with a quarter of the veggies and a quarter of the pepper Jack cheese. Use toothpicks to secure the sides of the chicken breast closed. Rub some of the spice mixture all over each chicken breast.

Place the chicken breasts in the air fryer basket. Spray the chicken with the spray oil.

Air-fry the chicken at 350°F (177°C) for 12 to 15 minutes.

Serve the chicken with the salsa, sour cream and guacamole on top.

Spray oil

1 tbsp (15 g) butter

1 small green bell pepper, thinly sliced

1 small red bell pepper, thinly sliced

1 small onion, thinly sliced

4 (4-oz [113-g]) boneless, skinless chicken breasts

2 tsp (6 g) chili powder

1 tsp garlic salt

1 tsp paprika

1 tsp sugar

½ tsp onion powder

⅛ tsp cayenne pepper

⅛ tsp black pepper

½ tsp ground cumin

1 cup (112 g) shredded pepper Jack cheese

Salsa, to serve

Sour cream, to serve

Guacamole, to serve

CHEESESTEAK-STUFFED PEPPERS

My family loves cheesesteaks, and these Cheesesteak-Stuffed Peppers bring all that cheesesteak flavor without all the bread. The cheesesteak filling cooks right in the bell peppers, giving the beef so much flavor.

Cut off the tops of 4 of the bell peppers and take out the seeds. Thinly slice the remaining bell pepper and set it aside.

In a large skillet over medium heat, cook the beef for 8 to 10 minutes, breaking it apart as it cooks. Drain off any grease. Add the paprika, garlic salt, black pepper and Worcestershire sauce. Remove the beef from the skillet. Return the skillet to medium heat.

In the skillet, combine the butter, sliced green bell pepper and onion. Sauté the bell pepper and onion for 10 to 15 minutes, until the vegetables are tender and caramelized. Return the beef to the skillet and stir to combine it with the onion and bell pepper.

In the bottom of each of the 4 bell peppers, place a scoop of the filling. Put 1 slice of provolone cheese in each bell pepper. Divide the rest of the filling among the bell peppers.

Air-fry the bell peppers at 355°F (179°C) for 10 minutes. Open the air fryer and carefully top each bell pepper with a slice of provolone cheese.

Air-fry the bell peppers at 355°F (179°C) for 5 more minutes.

MAKES: 4 SERVINGS

5 medium green bell peppers, divided

1 lb (454 g) ground beef

1 tbsp (9 g) paprika

1 tsp garlic salt

½ tsp black pepper

2 tbsp (30 ml) Worcestershire sauce

1 tbsp (15 g) butter

1 onion, thinly sliced

8 slices provolone cheese, divided

BUTTERMILK RANCH DRUMSTICKS

Not only are these Buttermilk Ranch Drumsticks flavorful and quick, they are super cheap to make! Chicken legs are so affordable, and you can get a ton of them for next to nothing. I give them a little buttermilk soak and ranch flavoring and roast them in my air fryer. Serve these with some mashed potatoes and you'll have one happy family.

In a gallon (3.8-L) ziplock bag, combine the buttermilk, ranch dressing mix, black pepper and chicken legs. Let the chicken marinate for 20 minutes.

Remove the chicken legs from the marinade and place them in the air fryer. Air-fry the chicken legs at 400°F (204°C) for 10 minutes. Flip the chicken legs and air-fry them at 400°F (204°C) for another 10 minutes.

Check that the chicken's internal temperature has reached 165°F (74°C). If not, air-fry it at 400°F (204°C) for 1 to 2 more minutes and check again.

**MAKES:
4 SERVINGS**

1 cup (240 ml) buttermilk

1 (1-oz [28-g]) packet ranch dressing mix

½ tsp black pepper

8 chicken legs

SPICY BROWN SUGAR SALMON

Nowadays, I never make my salmon in anything other than my air fryer. It comes out perfect every time. I eat a lot of salmon, so I have to switch up the flavors every now and then. I am really liking this Spicy Brown Sugar Salmon. It strikes a great balance between sweet and spicy.

Spray the air fryer basket with the spray oil.

In a small bowl, mix together the brown sugar, chili powder and cayenne pepper. Rub the spice mix all over each piece of salmon.

Place the salmon in the air fryer, skin side down. Air-fry the salmon at 355°F (179°C) for 15 minutes.

TIP: You can use skinless salmon, but I like to use the skin-on variety because it helps keep the fish from sticking to the air fryer basket.

MAKES:
4 SERVINGS

Spray oil

½ cup (72 g) brown sugar

½ tbsp (5 g) chili powder

½ tsp cayenne pepper

4 (4-oz [113-g]) skin-on salmon fillets

FRIED CABBAGE AND SAUSAGE

Fried cabbage is so, so good! I enjoy cooking with cabbage, and thankfully, my family loves it. This cabbage dish is seasoned with onion and cooks with smoked sausage, which helps flavor the cabbage.

In a large bowl, mix together the oil, salt and black pepper. Add the cabbage, onion and sausage and stir to coat.

Place the cabbage mixture in the air fryer and air-fry it at 400°F (204°C) for 10 minutes, stirring frequently.

TIP: You can save time and buy shredded coleslaw cabbage.

MAKES: 4 SERVINGS

1 tbsp (15 ml) oil of choice

½ tsp salt

½ tsp black pepper

½ small head cabbage, cored and coarsely chopped

1 small onion, thinly sliced

1 lb (454 g) smoked sausage, cut into bite-sized pieces

MAPLE-GLAZED PORK CHOPS

Pork chops are usually a quick item to cook, but they cook even faster in the air fryer, which makes them perfect for easy dinners. I love a little sweetness with my pork, and these Maple-Glazed Pork Chops are out of this world.

In a medium bowl, mix together the maple syrup, brown sugar, mustard, paprika and black pepper. Rub the maple syrup mixture all over both sides of the pork chops and place them in the air fryer.

Air-fry the pork chops at 400°F (204°C) for 6 minutes. Flip the pork chops and air-fry them at 400°F (204°C) for another 6 minutes.

MAKES:
4 SERVINGS

½ cup (120 ml) pure maple syrup

¼ cup (36 g) packed brown sugar

1 tbsp (15 g) Dijon mustard

¼ tsp paprika

¼ tsp black pepper

4 (1-inch [2.5-cm]) thick pork chops

SHREDDED CHICKEN AND SALSA QUESADILLAS

I always have leftover chicken or rotisserie chicken on hand, which allows these Shredded Chicken and Salsa Quesadillas to come together in minutes. Salsa, cheese and chicken is all you really need to make some amazing and quick quesadillas that even picky eaters will love.

In a medium bowl, mix together the chicken, salsa and green onion.

Spray the bottom of the air fryer basket with the spray oil and place a tortilla in the air fryer basket.

Top the tortilla with ⅛ cup (14 g) of the Colby Jack cheese and ¼ cup (31 g) of the chicken. Top the chicken with another ⅛ cup (14 g) of cheese. Top the filling with another tortilla and spray the top of the quesadilla with the spray oil.

Air-fry the quesadilla at 370°F (188°C) for 3 to 4 minutes. Flip the quesadilla and air-fry it for another 3 to 4 minutes. Repeat this process with the remaining ingredients.

Cut the quesadillas into quarters and serve them with the sour cream.

TIP: You can add anything you like to these quesadillas. Try various veggies, jalapeños or beans.

MAKES: 4 SERVINGS

2 cups (250 g) shredded cooked chicken

½ cup (120 ml) salsa

2 tbsp (12 g) coarsely chopped green onion

Spray oil

8 (8-inch [20-cm]) tortillas

2 cups (224 g) shredded Colby Jack cheese

Sour cream, to serve

CHIPOTLE BEEF MELTS

These are some of my favorite sandwiches. Roast beef, Cheddar cheese and chipotle sauce nestled within a croissant get warm and melty in the air fryer. This is another superquick meal that is great for dinner, for lunch or for a crowd. Everyone loves these flavorful sandwiches!

Slice the croissants in half.

In a small bowl, combine the mayonnaise with the adobo sauce. Spread a little of the chipotle mayonnaise on the bottom half of each croissant. Top each croissant slice with a slice of Cheddar cheese.

Divide the roast beef among the sandwiches. Top each one with a slice of pepper Jack cheese.

Spread the rest of the chipotle mayonnaise on the top half of each croissant. Make sandwiches by stacking the top half of the croissant over the bottom. Wrap the sandwiches in foil.

Place two sandwiches in the air fryer and air-fry them at 370°F (188°C) for 8 minutes, flipping them once during the cooking time. Repeat this process with the other two sandwiches.

TIP: You can add more adobo sauce to the mayonnaise if you like a little more kick.

MAKES:
4 SERVINGS

8 croissants

½ cup (110 g) mayonnaise

1 tbsp (15 ml) adobo sauce from chipotles in adobo

4 slices Cheddar cheese

8 oz (227 g) deli roast beef

4 slices pepper Jack cheese

HAM AND PINEAPPLE FRIED RICE

Fried rice in the air fryer? Of course! This Ham and Pineapple Fried Rice is a great way to use leftover ham. The pineapple gives the dish a sweet bite that goes so well with the salty ham and savory soy sauce.

In a large bowl, mix together the oil, soy sauce, salt and black pepper. Add the green onions, ham, peas, carrots, corn, pineapple and rice. Toss the ingredients gently until everything is combined.

Pour the rice in a deep baking dish that fits in the air fryer.

Air-fry the rice at 360°F (182°C) for 12 to 15 minutes, stirring frequently.

Meanwhile, melt the butter in a small skillet over medium heat. Add the eggs. Scramble the eggs for 3 to 5 minutes, until they are cooked through.

Remove the rice from the air fryer and stir in the eggs.

MAKES: 4 TO 6 SERVINGS

2 tbsp (30 ml) oil of choice

3 tbsp (45 ml) low-sodium soy sauce

1 tsp salt

½ tsp black pepper

4 green onions, coarsely chopped

2 cups (300 g) cubed ham

½ cup (75 g) frozen peas

½ cup (25 g) shredded carrots

½ cup (72 g) frozen corn

½ cup (122 g) pineapple tidbits in juice, drained

4 cups (640 g) cooked white or brown rice

1 tbsp (15 g) butter

4 large eggs, beaten

DECONSTRUCTED STEAK FAJITAS

Tender steak and fajita veggies are topped with a little cheese and served over rice with your favorite toppings like salsa, sour cream and guacamole. There's no need for tortillas here with all this flavor.

Lightly spray the air fryer basket with the spray oil.

Place the green bell pepper, red bell pepper and onion in the air fryer. Air-fry them at 400°F (204°C) for 5 minutes.

Meanwhile, mix together the chili powder, garlic salt, paprika, sugar, onion powder, cayenne pepper, black pepper, cumin, oil and garlic in a large bowl. Add the steak and toss to coat it in the seasoning.

Place the steak in the air fryer with the bell peppers and onion.

Air-fry the fajitas at 400°F (204°C) for 4 minutes. Immediately top the fajitas with the Monterey Jack cheese so it will melt.

Serve the fajitas with the salsa, sour cream and guacamole.

MAKES: 4 SERVINGS

Spray oil, as needed

1 medium green bell pepper, thinly sliced

1 medium red bell pepper, thinly sliced

1 small red onion, thinly sliced

2 tsp (6 g) chili powder

1 tsp garlic salt

1 tsp paprika

1 tsp sugar

½ tsp onion powder

⅛ tsp cayenne pepper

⅛ tsp black pepper

½ tsp ground cumin

1 tbsp (15 ml) oil of choice

2 cloves garlic, minced

1 lb (454 g) skirt or flank steak, thinly sliced against the grain

1 cup (112 g) shredded Monterey Jack cheese

Salsa, to serve

Sour cream, to serve

Guacamole, to serve

GREEN CHILI CHICKEN PIZZA

These mini pizzas are super fun to make and a nice change from your usual pepperoni and tomato sauce. This Green Chili Chicken Pizza is the perfect combination of pepper Jack cheese, shredded chicken and green chilis. Pizza cooks nicely in the air fryer and is ready in no time, making this a quick lunch or dinner.

Spread ¼ cup (60 ml) of the enchilada sauce on each pizza crust. Put ½ cup (63 g) of the shredded chicken on each crust. Sprinkle a quarter of the green chilis on each pizza. Top each pizza with ¼ cup (28 g) of the pepper Jack cheese and ¼ cup (28 g) of the Colby Jack cheese.

Working in batches, air-fry one pizza at 375°F (191°C) for 5 to 7 minutes. Repeat this process with the remaining pizzas.

MAKES:
4 SERVINGS

1 cup (240 ml) green enchilada sauce

4 mini pizza crusts

2 cups (250 g) shredded cooked chicken

1 (4-oz [113-g]) can diced green chilis, drained

1 cup (113 g) shredded pepper Jack cheese

1 cup (113 g) shredded Colby Jack cheese

ITALIAN SAUSAGE—STUFFED ZUCCHINI

There is always an abundance of zucchini in the summer, and I try to find ways to use it up. Stuffing it with Italian sausage and Parmesan cheese and cooking it in the air fryer is one of my favorite ways to serve zucchini. This is a fast and light dinner.

Scoop out the insides of the zucchini.

In a medium skillet over medium heat, cook the sausage for 8 to 10 minutes, breaking it apart as it cooks, until it is browned. Add the garlic, onion, salt and black pepper and cook the mixture for 5 minutes, just until the onion is soft.

In a medium bowl, combine the sausage-onion mixture, Parmesan cheese, ½ cup (56 g) of the mozzarella cheese and bread crumbs. Stir to combine the ingredients.

Fill the zucchini with the sausage mixture. Working in batches if necessary, place the stuffed zucchini in the air fryer and air-fry them at 350°F (177°C) for 10 minutes.

Top the zucchini with the remaining ½ cup (56 g) of mozzarella cheese. Air-fry them at 350°F (177°C) for 5 minutes.

Top the stuffed zucchini with the parsley (if using).

MAKES: 4 TO 6 SERVINGS

4 medium zucchini, cut in half lengthwise

1 lb (454 g) sweet Italian sausage

2 cloves garlic, minced

1 small onion, finely chopped

¼ tsp salt

¼ tsp black pepper

½ cup (90 g) grated Parmesan cheese

1 cup (112 g) shredded mozzarella cheese, divided

¼ cup (30 g) traditional bread crumbs

Finely chopped fresh parsley, to serve (optional)

HAM AND SWISS POCKETS
WITH HONEY MUSTARD SAUCE

These Ham and Swiss Pockets are similar to that microwave snack but are much better homemade. Ham and Swiss cheese meet a great honey mustard sauce and bake up in a flaky pocket right in the air fryer.

Unroll the pizza dough and cut it into four rectangles. Place ½ cup (75 g) of the ham in each rectangle. Place ½ cup (63 g) of the Swiss cheese in each rectangle.

In a small bowl, mix together the mustard and honey. Spoon the honey mustard all over each rectangle.

Fold the dough over and crimp the edges with a fork. Brush the tops of the pockets with the egg.

Working in batches if necessary, place the pockets in the air fryer and air-fry them at 360°F (182°C) for 10 minutes.

MAKES:
4 POCKETS

1 (14-oz [397-g]) package refrigerated pizza dough

2 cups (300 g) cubed ham

2 cups (250 g) coarsely chopped Swiss cheese

¼ cup (60 g) Dijon mustard

3 tbsp (45 ml) honey

1 large egg, beaten

BARBECUE CHICKEN PITA PIZZA

Pita bread makes an amazing pizza crust, so I always keep it on hand. I make this Barbecue Chicken Pita Pizza with chicken, barbecue sauce, onions, cheese—all that good stuff. These are easy and fast to make and my favorite kind of pizza.

Measure ½ cup (120 ml) of the barbecue sauce in a small measuring cup. Spread 2 tablespoons (30 ml) of the barbecue sauce on each pita.

In a medium bowl, mix together the remaining ½ cup (120 ml) of barbecue sauce and chicken. Place ½ cup (63 g) of the chicken on each pita. Top each pizza with ½ cup (56 g) of the mozzarella cheese. Sprinkle the tops of the pizzas with the red onion.

Place one pizza in the air fryer. Air-fry the pizza at 400°F (204°C) for 5 to 7 minutes. Repeat this process with the remaining pizzas.

Top the pizzas with the cilantro.

TIP: Try adding a little pineapple before cooking—it's delicious!

MAKES: 4 PIZZAS

1 cup (240 ml) barbecue sauce, divided

4 pita breads

2 cups (250 g) shredded cooked chicken

2 cups (224 g) shredded mozzarella cheese

½ small red onion, thinly sliced

2 tbsp (6 g) finely chopped fresh cilantro

GREEN CHILI CHICKEN TAQUITOS

There is nothing better than a crispy taquito, and you can get the crispiest taquito ready for dunking right from your air fryer. I fill these taquitos with plenty of cheese, chicken and green chilis.

Spray the basket of the air fryer with the spray oil.

In a medium bowl, mix together the chicken, Colby Jack cheese, pepper Jack cheese, green chilis and corn. Divide the chicken mixture among the tortillas.

Roll up the tortillas. Working in batches, if necessary, place the taquitos seam side down in the air fryer. Spray the tops of the taquitos with the spray oil and sprinkle them with a little kosher salt.

Air-fry the taquitos at 400°F (204°C) for 8 minutes.

Serve the taquitos with the sour cream for dipping.

TIP: Switch out the chicken for black beans if you want a meatless option.

MAKES:
2 TO 4 SERVINGS

Spray oil

2 cups (250 g) shredded cooked chicken

1 cup (112 g) shredded Colby Jack cheese

1 cup (112 g) shredded pepper Jack cheese

2 tbsp (30 g) canned diced roasted green chilis, drained

¼ cup (36 g) drained canned, frozen or fresh corn

8 (6-inch [15-cm]) flour tortillas

Kosher salt

Sour cream, to serve

KOREAN CHICKEN WINGS

Chicken wings come out perfect every time in the air fryer. You can season them any way you like, but I really enjoy these Korean Chicken Wings. They marinate quickly before getting crispy in the air fryer.

In a gallon (3.8-L) ziplock bag, combine the soy sauce, vinegar, brown sugar, cola, garlic and green onion. Add the chicken wings to the bag. Lay the bag flat and marinate the chicken for 30 minutes. Flip the bag over and marinate the chicken for another 30 minutes.

Remove all the wings from the bag and place them in the air fryer in a single layer. Air-fry the chicken wings at 360°F (182°C) for 12 minutes. Flip the wings and air-fry them at 360°F (182°C) for another 12 minutes.

**MAKES:
2 TO 4 SERVINGS**

¾ cup (180 ml) soy sauce

1 tbsp (15 ml) rice wine vinegar

1 cup (144 g) brown sugar

¾ cup (180 ml) cola

2 cloves garlic, finely chopped

2 tbsp (12 g) coarsely chopped green onion

2 lbs (900 g) chicken wings

JAMAICAN JERK CHICKEN FRIED RICE

Jamaican Jerk Chicken Fried Rice is a flavor explosion. Blackened chicken tenders, veggies, rice and beans all come together in the air fryer to create the perfect blend of flavors in a quick, tasty dinner.

Chicken

2 tsp (6 g) ground allspice

2 tbsp (18 g) brown sugar

¼ tsp ground cinnamon

1 tsp salt

½ tsp black pepper

⅛ tsp cayenne pepper

3 green onions, coarsely chopped

2 cloves garlic, minced

⅛ tsp ground ginger

2 tbsp (30 ml) fresh lime juice

2 tbsp (30 ml) soy sauce

1 tsp dried thyme

1 tbsp (15 ml) oil of choice

1 lb (454 g) boneless, skinless chicken tenderloins

Spray oil

**MAKES:
4 SERVINGS**

Fried Rice

2 cups (320 g) cooked white rice

2 green onions, coarsely chopped

¼ tsp black pepper

2 tbsp (30 ml) soy sauce

½ tsp sesame oil

½ cup (25 g) shredded carrots

1 clove garlic, minced

2 tbsp (30 ml) vegetable oil

½ cup (88 g) diced red bell pepper

½ cup (75 g) frozen peas

½ cup (30 g) black beans, drained and rinsed

To make the chicken, combine the allspice, brown sugar, cinnamon, salt, black pepper, cayenne pepper, green onions, garlic, ginger, lime juice, soy sauce, thyme and oil in a food processor. Process the ingredients until they are well combined. Pour the marinade into a gallon (3.8-L) ziplock bag and add the chicken tenderloins.

Let the chicken marinate for 1 hour.

Spray the air fryer basket with the spray oil. Place the chicken tenderloins in the basket. Spray the chicken with additional spray oil.

Air-fry the chicken at 360°F (182°C) for 8 to 10 minutes, until the chicken's internal temperature reaches 165°F (74°C).

Set the chicken aside until it's cool enough to handle.

To make the fried rice, cut the chicken into small pieces. Transfer the chicken to a large bowl and add the rice, green onions, black pepper, soy sauce, sesame oil, carrots, garlic, vegetable oil, bell pepper, peas and black beans. Toss to combine the ingredients.

Place all of the fried rice in a baking dish that will fit in the air fryer basket. Air-fry the rice at 360°F (182°F) for 20 minutes, stirring frequently.

TIP: You can add pineapple or mango to the rice for a little pop of sweetness.

PULLED PORK BUNS

Where I am from, we eat our pork with vinegar-based Carolina-style sauce. I like to stuff the pork in biscuit dough with a little coleslaw and bake it in the air fryer for an exciting meal everyone falls in love with.

In a large bowl, combine the cabbage, oil, vinegar, sugar, black pepper and celery seeds. Set the coleslaw aside to marinate.

Meanwhile, lay out the biscuits on a work surface and lightly flatten each one. Place 1 tablespoon (16 g) of the pork on each biscuit and top the pork with 1 tablespoon (21 g) of the coleslaw. Pull up the sides of the dough and pinch the dough around the top like a purse.

Brush all the buns with the beaten egg.

Air-fry the buns at 360°F (182°C) for 5 minutes.

MAKES:
4 TO 6 SERVINGS

½ small head cabbage, shredded

2 tbsp (30 ml) vegetable or canola oil

2 tbsp (30 ml) distilled white vinegar

2 tbsp (24 g) sugar

¼ tsp black pepper

¼ tsp celery seeds

1 (1-lb [454-g]) can jumbo biscuits

2 cups (500 g) Carolina-style pulled pork or pulled pork of choice

1 large egg, beaten

LOADED CHICKEN NACHOS

I couldn't have a chapter of quick and easy meals without some nachos! These Loaded Chicken Nachos are just that: loaded with flavor and toppings. I top my chips with chicken, corn, black beans and cheese and let the nachos get melty in the air fryer, then we go crazy with the toppings. Salsa, guacamole, roasted veggies, sour cream—you can load up on any of your favorites. These are great when you are feeding a crowd!

Place a parchment round in the bottom of the air fryer basket.

In a medium bowl, toss the chicken with the taco seasoning.

Place 4 cups (100 g) of the chips in the air fryer basket. Top the chips with 1 cup (125 g) of the chicken, ¼ cup (36 g) of the corn, ¼ cup (15 g) black of the beans, 1 cup (112 g) of the Colby Jack cheese and 1 tablespoon (6 g) of the green onion.

Air-fry the nachos at 350°F (177°C) for 5 minutes.

Transfer the nachos to a platter and repeat this process with the remaining ingredients.

Top the nachos with the salsa, sour cream and guacamole.

TIP: Add jalapeños for some heat!

MAKES:
4 SERVINGS

2 cups (250 g) shredded cooked chicken

2 tsp (6 g) taco seasoning

8 cups (200 g) tortilla chips

½ cup (72 g) drained canned, frozen or fresh corn

½ cup (30 g) canned black beans, drained and rinsed

2 cups (224 g) shredded Colby Jack cheese

2 tbsp (12 g) coarsely chopped green onion

½ cup (120 ml) salsa

½ cup (60 g) sour cream

½ cup (240 g) guacamole

FALAFEL

Falafel are great to make in the air fryer—they come out crisp every time. These are another quick and easy meatless option. We enjoy ours in pita bread with a little hummus, lettuce and tomato.

To make the falafel, place a parchment round in the air fryer basket and spray it with the spray oil.

In a food processor, combine the chickpeas, onion, parsley, cilantro, salt, cayenne pepper, garlic, cumin and baking powder. Pulse until the ingredients just come together. Add the flour, 1 tablespoon (8 g) at a time, and pulse until the mixture forms a thick paste (you don't want it to be completely smooth).

Roll the falafel mixture into 1- to 1½-inch (2.5- to 4-cm) disks. Place a single layer of falafel in the air fryer and spritz them with more spray oil.

Air-fry the falafel at 350°F (177°C) for 7 minutes. Flip the falafel and air-fry them at 350°F (177°C) for another 7 minutes. Repeat this process with the remaining falafel.

To make the sandwiches, pile the falafel into the pitas with the hummus, cucumber, lettuce, tomato and onion.

MAKES:
5 TO 6 SERVINGS

Falafel
Spray oil

1 cup (165 g) canned chickpeas, drained

½ small onion, diced

2 tbsp (6 g) coarsely chopped fresh parsley

2 tbsp (6 g) coarsely chopped fresh cilantro

1 tsp salt

¼ tsp cayenne pepper

4 cloves garlic

1 tsp ground cumin

1 tsp baking powder

4 to 6 tbsp (32 to 48 g) all-purpose flour

Sandwiches
Pita breads

Hummus

Thinly sliced cucumber

Lettuce leaves

Thinly sliced tomato

Thinly sliced red onion

CAJUN SHRIMP, SAUSAGE AND POTATOES

Shrimp is a great choice when you are looking to get a meal on the table quickly. This recipe is inspired by big shrimp boils, except we are cooking this in the air fryer with Cajun-seasoned shrimp, sausage and potatoes.

In a large bowl, combine the potatoes, onion, Cajun seasoning, garlic salt and 1 tablespoon (15 ml) of the oil.

Place the potatoes in the air fryer and air-fry them at 400°F (177°C) for 6 minutes.

Pull out the air fryer basket and add the sausage. Air-fry the mixture at 400°F (177°C) for 4 minutes.

Meanwhile, in a medium bowl, toss the shrimp with the remaining 1 tablespoon (15 ml) of oil and the seafood seasoning. Add the shrimp to the air fryer with the sausage and potatoes and air-fry the mixture at 400°F (177°C) for 6 minutes.

TIP: You can add some corn on the cob, as well, if you cut the ears of corn into smaller pieces. Add the corn when you add the sausage.

MAKES: 4 SERVINGS

1 lb (450 g) baby potatoes, quartered

½ small onion, coarsely chopped

1 tsp Cajun seasoning

½ tsp garlic salt

2 tbsp (30 ml) oil of choice, divided

8 oz (224 g) Cajun-style andouille sausage, thickly sliced

1 lb (450 g) large raw shrimp, peeled and deveined

2 tsp (6 g) seafood seasoning

OLD BAY CRISPY SHRIMP

My mom loves shrimp and she loves Old Bay Seasoning with her crabs, so why not combine the two into one crispy dish? Shrimp cooks so fast and gets so crispy in the air fryer, you can have this on the table in minutes.

Place a parchment round in the bottom of the air fryer basket and spritz it with the spray oil.

In a shallow dish, mix together the flour, cornmeal and Old Bay Seasoning. Place the eggs in another shallow dish.

Dip the shrimp in the eggs and then into the breading. Place a single layer of shrimp in the air fryer and spray them with the spray oil.

Air-fry the shrimp at 375°F (191°C) for 8 minutes, flipping them halfway through the cooking time. Repeat the process with the remaining shrimp.

Serve the shrimp with the cocktail sauce and lemon wedges.

MAKES:
4 SERVINGS

Spray oil

¼ cup (30 g) all-purpose flour

¼ cup (43 g) cornmeal

1 tsp Old Bay Seasoning

2 large eggs, beaten

1 lb (454 g) raw shrimp, peeled and deveined

Cocktail sauce, to serve

Lemon wedges, to serve

CRISPY ITALIAN PORK CHOPS

Anytime you need a quick and easy dinner, pork chops are always the way to go. These Crispy Italian Pork Chops are divine. Seasoned with garlic and Italian dressing, they also get a salty bite from Parmesan cheese in the breading. They are really tasty.

Place a parchment round in the air fryer basket and spritz it with the spray oil.

Place the flour in a shallow dish. In a second shallow dish, beat the eggs with the Italian dressing. In a third shallow dish, mix together the panko bread crumbs, garlic salt, black pepper and Parmesan cheese.

Coat the pork chops with the flour, then dip them into the egg mixture, then into the panko bread crumbs.

Place the pork chops in the air fryer. Air-fry them at 325°F (163°C) for 10 minutes. Flip the pork chops and air-fry at 325°F (163°C) for 8 to 10 minutes.

MAKES:
4 SERVINGS

Spray oil

4 tbsp (32 g) all-purpose flour

2 large eggs

2 tbsp (30 ml) Italian dressing

2 cups (110 g) Italian-seasoned panko bread crumbs

½ tsp garlic salt

½ tsp black pepper

3 tbsp (33 g) grated Parmesan cheese

4 (1-inch [2.5-cm]-thick) boneless pork chops

PINEAPPLE BARBECUE PORK BITES

This is another one of my family's favorite quick dinners. Pineapple Barbecue Pork Bites are sweet with a little spice from the barbecue sauce. These sticky, tender morsels are perfect on top of a bed of rice.

**MAKES:
4 SERVINGS**

Spray oil

½ cup (120 ml) barbecue sauce

¼ cup (60 ml) pineapple juice

2 tbsp (18 g) brown sugar or 2 tbsp (30 ml) honey

1 lb (454 g) pork chops or pork tenderloin, cut into bite-sized pieces

¼ cup (61 g) pineapple tidbits

Cooked white rice, to serve

Place a parchment round in the bottom of the air fryer basket and spritz it with the spray oil.

In a large bowl, combine the barbecue sauce, pineapple juice and brown sugar. Add the pork and pineapple tidbits and toss them in the sauce to coat them.

Remove the pork bites and pineapple from the marinade liquid and place them in the air fryer. Discard the leftover marinade. Air-fry them at 400°F (204°C) for 8 to 10 minutes, flipping them once during the cooking time. (If the pork bites aren't done at the end of the cooking time, air-fry them for 1 to 2 minutes more.)

Serve the pork bites over the rice.

FAMILY FAVORITES

These recipes are tried-and-true favorites, real crowd-pleasers, dishes even your pickiest eaters will love. They are comforting, familiar dishes that can be made quickly in the air fryer, things like Crispy Chicken Fries (page 316) and Corn Dog Muffins (page 347), which my kids love and I make weekly. We love having family-friendly meals like The Best Rotisserie Chicken (page 339) and Cheesy Baked Ziti (page 351). So if you are looking for meals the whole family will love, look no further!

CRISPY CHICKEN FRIES

My youngest loves chicken fries—he could eat them every day. We love them because they are super crispy and perfect for dipping in our favorite sauces. These cook quickly in the air fryer, which is something to be thankful for because you will be making them often!

Place a parchment round in the air fryer basket and spritz it with the spray oil.

In a shallow dish, mix together the flour, garlic salt, black pepper, paprika and onion powder. Place the eggs in a second shallow dish. Combine the panko bread crumbs and traditional bread crumbs in a third shallow dish.

Coat each of the chicken strips in the flour mixture, then dip them in the eggs, then coat them in the bread crumbs.

Place half of the chicken strips in the air fryer and spray them with the spray oil.

Air-fry the chicken strips at 390°F (199°C) for 3 minutes. Flip the chicken strips and air-fry them at 390°F (199°C) for another 3 minutes. Repeat this process with the remaining chicken strips.

TIP: Add 1 tablespoon (15 ml) of hot sauce to the eggs to give these chicken fries a spicy kick.

MAKES:
4 SERVINGS

Spray oil

1 cup (120 g) all-purpose flour

1 tsp garlic salt

½ tsp black pepper

½ tsp paprika

½ tsp onion powder

2 large eggs, beaten

2 cups (110 g) panko bread crumbs

½ cup (60 g) traditional bread crumbs

1 lb (454 g) boneless, skinless chicken breasts, cut into thin strips

STUFFED SHELLS WITH MEAT SAUCE

Everyone gets excited when they see this steamy pan of cheesy Stuffed Shells with Meat Sauce on the dinner table. Pasta shells filled with mozzarella and ricotta are topped with a hearty meat sauce. These cook up in minutes in the air fryer and make a fabulous meal with a salad and some bread.

Bring a large pot of salted water to a boil over high heat. Add the pasta shells and boil them for about 8 minutes, until they are al dente. Drain and rinse them under cold water. Set them aside.

Meanwhile, in a medium skillet over medium heat, cook the Italian sausage for 8 to 10 minutes, breaking it apart as it cooks, until it is browned. Add the pasta sauce to the sausage and remove the skillet from the heat.

In a medium bowl, mix together the ricotta cheese, egg, 1½ cups (168 g) of the mozzarella cheese and the Parmesan cheese.

Spread about ¼ cup (60 ml) of the meat sauce in the bottom of a 1½-quart (1.4-L) baking dish.

Fill the pasta shells with the cheese mixture and place them in the baking dish. Top the shells with the rest of the meat sauce and the remaining ½ cup (56 g) of mozzarella cheese.

Cover the baking dish with foil and air-fry the stuffed shells at 300°F (149°C) for 20 minutes. Remove the foil and air-fry the shells at 300°F (149°C) for 2 to 3 minutes to melt the cheese.

TIP: Add cooked, drained spinach to the ricotta mixture—it's delicious!

MAKES:
4 SERVINGS

1 (12-oz [340-g]) box jumbo pasta shells

1 lb (454 g) ground Italian sausage

1 (26-oz [737-ml]) jar pasta sauce

2 cups (246 g) ricotta cheese

1 large egg

2 cups (224 g) shredded mozzarella cheese, divided

¼ cup (45 g) grated Parmesan cheese

SPICY CHEESY HOT DOGS

My grandma taught me how to make the best hot dogs. I bet you didn't know you could take hot dogs to the next level while cooking them, but you can, and I do it in the air fryer to save time! These hot dogs are split and roasted with butter and hot sauce before being filled with melty cheese.

Split the hot dogs down the middle, being careful not to cut all the way through.

In a small microwave-safe bowl, combine the butter and hot sauce. Microwave the mixture for 30 seconds, until the butter has melted.

Place the hot dogs in the air fryer and spoon the butter–hot sauce mixture over all the hot dogs. Air-fry the hot dogs at 390°F (199°C) for 6 minutes.

Remove the hot dogs from the air fryer and place them in the hot dog buns. Return the hot dogs to the air fryer and fill each one with the Cheddar cheese.

Air-fry the hot dogs at 390°F (199°C) for 2 minutes, until the cheese has melted.

TIP: These are the perfect base for all of your favorite hot dog toppings.

MAKES:
8 HOT DOGS

8 hot dogs

1 tbsp (15 g) butter

1 tbsp (15 ml) hot sauce

8 hot dog buns

1 cup (120 g) shredded Cheddar cheese

SUNDAY SPECIAL CHICKEN SANDWICH

Ever crave a certain drive-through chicken sandwich only to realize it's Sunday and the restaurant is closed? Happens to me all the time, which is why I always keep this recipe for my Sunday Special Chicken Sandwich on hand. It tastes just like the one you're craving but it's better for you since you are air-frying it instead of deep-frying it. Just make sure to throw some waffle fries in the air fryer too!

Pound the chicken breasts until they are roughly half their original thickness.

In a large bowl, mix together the milk and pickle brine. Add the chicken and let it marinate for 30 minutes.

In a food processor, combine the crackers, bread crumbs, flour, paprika, black pepper, salt and powdered sugar. Pulse until the mixture has a fine texture.

Spray the bottom of the air fryer basket with the spray oil.

Remove the chicken from the marinade and dredge the chicken in the cracker mixture, pressing the coating into the chicken.

Add the chicken pieces to the air fryer and air-fry them at 350°F (177°C) for 8 minutes. Flip the chicken pieces and air-fry them at 350°F (177°C) for 8 minutes.

Immediately place the hot chicken on the hamburger buns and add 2 pickle slices per sandwich.

MAKES: 4 SANDWICHES

4 (4-oz [113-g]) boneless, skinless chicken breasts

1½ cups (360 ml) milk

½ cup (120 ml) dill pickle brine

1 sleeve buttery crackers

1½ cups (180 g) traditional bread crumbs

½ cup (63 g) all-purpose flour

1½ tsp (5 g) paprika

1½ tsp (3 g) black pepper

2 tsp (10 g) salt

½ cup (65 g) powdered sugar

Spray oil

4 hamburger buns

8 slices dill pickles

BURGER AND TOT SKEWERS

Burgers and tots always make a fast dinner everyone loves. I like putting them together on a skewer, which makes them perfect for dipping. My kids really enjoy this dinner and so do I. These are a fun and different spin on your usual burger dinner.

In a medium bowl, combine the beef, Worcestershire sauce and steak seasoning. Roll the beef into 1½-inch (4-cm) meatballs.

Skewer the tater tots and meatballs, alternating between the tater tots and meatballs. Air-fry the skewers at 400°F (204°C) for 10 minutes, flipping the skewers once during the cooking time.

Pull the basket out of the air fryer. Place a quarter of a slice of American cheese on each meatball. Air-fry the skewers at 400°F (204°C) for 1 minute.

Drizzle the skewers with the ketchup and mustard.

TIP: Thread some red onion onto the skewers if you like onion on your burgers!

MAKES: 4 SERVINGS

1 lb (454 g) ground beef

½ tbsp (8 ml) Worcestershire sauce

½ tbsp (5 g) Montreal steak seasoning

½ (32-oz [907-g]) bag frozen tater tots, thawed

4 to 6 slices American cheese, quartered

Ketchup, to serve

Mustard, to serve

CHICKEN ALFREDO CALZONES

Calzones are always a hit in our house. These Chicken Alfredo Calzones are stuffed with tender chicken, ricotta cheese, Alfredo sauce and mozzarella. Bake them fast in the air fryer and you will have a happy family at the dinner table.

Roll out the pizza dough on a work surface. Cut the pizza dough into four rectangles. Shape each rectangle into a rough circle that can fit inside the air fryer.

In a medium bowl, combine the chicken with the Alfredo sauce.

Spread ¼ cup (31 g) of the ricotta cheese on each dough circle. Add ½ cup (63 g) of the chicken and sauce to each dough circle. Sprinkle ¼ cup (28 g) of the mozzarella cheese on each dough circle.

Fold each calzone in half and roll or pinch the edges closed.

In a small microwave-safe bowl, combine the butter and garlic salt. Microwave the mixture for 30 seconds, until the butter has melted.

Brush each calzone with the garlic butter. Sprinkle each calzone with the Parmesan cheese.

Air-fry the calzones at 325°F (163°C) for 12 minutes.

Serve the calzones while they are hot.

MAKES: 4 SERVINGS

1 (14-oz [397-g]) package refrigerated pizza dough

2 cups (250 g) shredded cooked chicken

1½ cups (360 ml) Alfredo sauce

1 cup (123 g) ricotta cheese

1 cup (112 g) shredded mozzarella cheese

2 tbsp (30 g) butter

1 tsp garlic salt

Grated Parmesan cheese

QUESADILLA BURRITO

Why choose between a quesadilla and a burrito when you can have both? A cheese quesadilla stuffed with all of your favorite burrito fillings makes a hearty and delicious dinner perfect for Taco Tuesday.

Spray the air fryer basket with the spray oil.

In a medium skillet over medium heat, cook the beef for 8 to 10 minutes, until it is browned. Drain any excess grease. Add the taco seasoning and ¼ cup (60 ml) of the water and stir to combine. Cook the beef for 2 to 3 minutes, then remove the skillet from the heat.

Meanwhile, in a medium saucepan over high heat, combine the rice, remaining 1 cup (240 ml) of water, garlic, tomato sauce and garlic salt. Bring the rice to a boil. Cover the saucepan and reduce the heat to low. Simmer the rice for 16 minutes.

Place ½ cup (56 g) of the Colby Jack cheese on 4 of the tortillas and top them with the remaining 4 tortillas.

Microwave each quesadilla for 30 seconds.

Place a quarter of the nacho cheese dip, a quarter of the meat and a quarter of the rice on top of each quesadilla.

Top each one with 1 tablespoon (8 g) of the sour cream. Fold in the sides of each quesadilla burrito and roll it up carefully.

Spray the air fryer with the spray oil and place two quesadilla burritos in the basket. Spray them with the spray oil. Air-fry the quesadilla burritos at 350°F (177°C) for 6 to 8 minutes.

Repeat this process with the remaining quesadilla burritos.

TIP: Replace the beef with chicken if you like. Feel free to add your favorite burrito toppings inside.

MAKES:
4 SERVINGS

Spray oil

1 lb (454 g) ground beef

1 (1-oz [28-g]) packet taco seasoning

1¼ cups (300 ml) water, divided

½ cup (210 g) white uncooked rice

1 clove garlic, minced

1 tbsp (15 ml) tomato sauce

½ tsp garlic salt

2 cups (224 g) shredded Colby Jack cheese

8 (10-inch [25-cm]) tortillas

1 cup (240 ml) nacho cheese dip

¼ cup (30 g) sour cream

CRUNCHY FISH STICKS

Fish sticks are my go-to when I need a quick lunch for me or my kids. These Crunchy Fish Sticks are a cinch to make and taste so fresh. We love dipping ours in ketchup or tartar sauce.

Spray the basket of the air fryer with the spray oil.

Cut the cod into 1 x 3–inch (2.5 x 7.5–cm) sticks.

Place the flour in a shallow dish. Place the egg in a second shallow dish. In the third shallow dish, combine the panko bread crumbs, paprika, salt and black pepper.

Coat each fish stick in the flour, then in the egg, then in the panko mixture.

Place half of the fish sticks in a single layer in the air fryer basket, making sure they are not touching. Spray the fish sticks with the spray oil.

Air-fry the fish sticks at 400°F (204°C) for 10 minutes, flipping them once halfway through the cooking time. Repeat this process with the remaining fish sticks.

TIP: You can use any whitefish to make your fish sticks.

**MAKES:
4 SERVINGS**

Spray oil

1 lb (454 g) cod fillets

¼ cup (30 g) all-purpose flour

1 large egg, beaten

1 cup (55 g) panko bread crumbs

1 tsp paprika

1 tsp salt

½ tsp black pepper

CHICKEN FAJITA GRILLED CHEESE

Why have a regular grilled cheese when you can have a Chicken Fajita Grilled Cheese? Fajita veggies and chicken come together with melty Cheddar and pepper Jack for the perfect grilled cheese. This one is fabulous dipped in tomato soup.

Melt 2 tablespoons (30 g) of the butter in a large skillet over medium heat. Add the bell pepper and onion. Cook them for 5 to 8 minutes, until the onion is translucent.

Add the chicken, cumin, garlic salt, black pepper and paprika. Cook the mixture for 10 minutes, until the chicken is cooked through. Remove the skillet from the heat and set it aside.

With the remaining 4 tablespoons (60 g) of butter, butter one side of each slice of bread. Place 2 pieces of bread in the air fryer, buttered side down. Place 1 slice of Cheddar cheese and a quarter of the fajita chicken mixture on each slice of bread. Top the fajita chicken mixture with 1 slice of pepper Jack cheese. Top the pepper Jack cheese with another slice of bread, buttered side up.

Air-fry the sandwiches at 350°F (177°C) for 8 minutes, flipping them once during the cooking time. Repeat this process with the remaining sandwiches.

Slice each sandwich in half prior to serving.

TIP: A good, thick bread is best for these loaded grilled cheese sandwiches.

MAKES:
4 SERVINGS

6 tbsp (90 g) butter, softened, divided

1 small green bell pepper, thinly sliced

1 small onion, thinly sliced

2 (4-oz [113-g]) boneless, skinless chicken breasts, thinly sliced

1 tsp ground cumin

1 tsp garlic salt

½ tsp black pepper

½ tsp paprika

8 slices bread

4 slices Cheddar cheese

4 slices pepper Jack cheese

WAFFLE FRY NACHOS

I love nachos. But put those nacho toppings on waffle fries and it's a life changer. Taco-spiced beef, queso cheese and all of your favorite toppings are amazing on top of crispy waffle fries!

In a medium skillet over medium heat, cook the beef for 8 to 10 minutes, breaking it apart as it cooks, until it is browned. Drain any grease. Add the taco seasoning, water and beans, stirring to combine the ingredients. Remove the skillet from the heat.

Meanwhile, place all the waffle fries in the air fryer and air-fry them at 400°F (204°C) for 15 minutes, shaking the air fryer basket once or twice.

Remove half of the waffle fries from the air fryer basket and set them aside.

Top the fries in the air fryer basket with half of the taco meat and 1 cup (120 g) of the Cheddar cheese.

Air-fry the nachos at 400°F (204°C) for 2 minutes. Remove the nachos and transfer them to a serving plate.

Place the remaining waffle fries in the air fryer and top them with the remaining taco meat and 1 cup (120 g) of Cheddar cheese. Air-fry the nachos at 400°F (204°C) for 2 minutes.

Top the waffle fry nachos with the green onion, sour cream and salsa.

MAKES:
4 SERVINGS

1 lb (454 g) ground beef

1 (1-oz [28-g]) packet taco seasoning

⅓ cup (80 ml) water

1 cup (60 g) black beans, drained and rinsed

1 (24-oz [680-g]) bag waffle fries

2 cups (240 g) shredded Cheddar cheese, divided

4 tbsp (24 g) coarsely chopped green onion

Sour cream, to serve

Salsa, to serve

EVERYTHING BAGEL CHEESE DOGS

This is a dinner I love to make when I want something super quick and super easy. It's a no-brainer dinner. Cheesy sausages are wrapped in flaky crescent roll dough and topped with everything bagel seasoning. Serve this with a quick side and you've got dinner in no time. These also make a great lunch.

Spritz the air fryer basket with the spray oil.

Unroll the crescent rolls from their cans. Pinch two of the crescent roll triangles together into a rectangle so that you have eight rectangles. In each rectangle, place 1 sausage and a sprinkling of the Cheddar cheese. Tuck in the ends of the dough and roll up the sausages in the dough.

Brush each cheese dog with butter and sprinkle each one with a bit of the Everything Bagel Seasoning.

Place four of the cheese dogs in the air fryer basket and air-fry them at 400°F (204°C) for 7 minutes. Repeat this process with the remaining cheese dogs.

TIP: These are great with mustard!

MAKES:
8 CHEESE DOGS

Spray oil

2 (8-oz [227-g]) cans crescent rolls

8 Cheddar smoked sausages

1 cup (120 g) shredded Cheddar cheese

2 tbsp (30 g) butter, melted

1 tbsp (9 g) Everything Bagel Seasoning (page 48)

THE BEST ROTISSERIE CHICKEN

I make this every Sunday—even if we don't eat it that day, I still make it, because I use that chicken all week for dinner. You will see a lot of recipes in this book that call for shredded chicken, and this is where I get mine. Why waste money buying precooked rotisserie chickens when you can make your own in the air fryer? I season mine simply, and it comes out moist with crispy skin. It is fabulous on top of mashed potatoes for dinner.

Spray the air fryer basket with the spray oil.

In a small bowl, combine the butter with the garlic salt, paprika, black pepper and dried minced onion. Brush the seasoned butter all over the chicken.

Place the chicken, breast side down, in the air fryer basket and air-fry it at 350°F (177°C) for 30 minutes. Flip the chicken so that it is breast side up. Air-fry the chicken at 350°F (177°C) for 20 to 25 minutes, until the chicken's internal temperature reaches 165°F (74°C).

MAKES: 4 TO 6 SERVINGS

Spray oil

2 tbsp (30 g) butter, melted

1 tsp garlic salt

1 tsp paprika

1 tsp black pepper

½ tsp dried minced onion or onion powder

1 (5-lb [2.3-kg]) whole chicken, giblets removed

SUPREME PIZZA QUESADILLAS

If you think all quesadillas have to be filled with taco meat or fajita chicken, think again! We love making pizza quesadillas in our house. These Supreme Pizza Quesadillas are filled with your favorite pizza toppings: Italian sausage, pepperoni, peppers, olives and lots of mozzarella cheese. Crisp these up in the air fryer and dunk them in pizza sauce for a dinner your family will flip for.

Spray the air fryer basket with the spray oil.

Spread 2 tablespoons (30 ml) of the pizza sauce on each of 4 tortillas. Place ½ cup (56 g) of the mozzarella cheese on each of the 4 tortillas. Divide the sausage, pepperoni, bell pepper, onion, olives (if using) and oregano among the tortillas. Top each with another tortilla.

Place one quesadilla in the air fryer and spray the top with the spray oil.

Air-fry the quesadilla at 320°F (160°C) for 6 minutes, flipping it halfway through the cooking time. Repeat this process with the remaining quesadillas.

Slice the quesadillas into quarters.

TIP: Serve this with extra marinara or ranch on the side!

MAKES: 4 SERVINGS

Spray oil, as needed

½ cup (120 ml) pizza or marinara sauce

8 (10-inch [25-cm]) tortillas

2 cups (224 g) shredded mozzarella cheese

1 cup (130 g) cooked and crumbled Italian sausage

20 pepperoni slices

1 small green bell pepper, thinly sliced

1 small onion, thinly sliced

4 tbsp (44 g) sliced black olives (optional)

½ tbsp (2 g) dried oregano

SPICY CHICKEN NUGGETS

Is there anyone that doesn't love chicken nuggets? Of course not! And these Spicy Chicken Nuggets are perfect if you want a little kick with your usual nuggets. These are perfect for dipping in ranch and are a quick dinner that will leave everyone happy.

Spray the air fryer basket with the spray oil. In a shallow dish, mix together the butter with the hot sauce and stir to combine. In a second shallow dish, mix together the bread crumbs, paprika, black pepper and garlic salt. Place all the nuggets in the butter–hot sauce mixture. Then coat the nuggets in the bread crumb mixture.

Place the nuggets in the air fryer in a single layer. Spray the nuggets with the spray oil.

Air-fry the nuggets at 390°F (199°C) for 6 to 9 minutes, flipping them once during the cooking time. Repeat this process with the remaining nuggets.

TIP: Serve these with blue cheese dressing, carrots and celery.

**MAKES:
4 SERVINGS**

Spray oil

3 tbsp (45 ml) melted butter, cooled

3 tbsp (45 ml) hot sauce

2 cups (240 g) traditional bread crumbs

1 tsp paprika

1 tsp coarse black pepper

½ tsp garlic salt

1 lb (454 g) boneless, skinless chicken tenderloins, cut into bite-sized pieces

CHILI CHEESEBURGER OVER FRIES

This meal is comfort on a plate. It is hearty, filling and so yummy. Crispy waffle fries are topped with a burger, chili and cheese. It is the perfect mixture of chili cheese fries and cheeseburger, all in one amazing dish.

In a medium bowl, mix together the beef, dried minced onion, Worcestershire sauce and steak seasoning. Divide the beef into four equal portions and shape them into patties.

Place two patties in the air fryer and air-fry them at 375°F (191°C) for 8 minutes, flipping them halfway through the cooking time. Repeat this process with the remaining burgers. Set the burgers aside.

Place all of the fries in the air fryer and air-fry them at 350°F (177°C) for 15 minutes, shaking the basket once or twice during the cooking time. Remove half of the fries from the air fryer basket and set them aside.

Place two burgers on top of the fries in the air fryer and sprinkle everything with ¾ cup (90 g) of the Cheddar cheese. Air-fry the burgers and fries at 350°F (177°C) for 2 to 3 minutes, until the cheese has melted. Remove the burgers and fries from the air fryer and repeat this process with the remaining fries, burgers and ¾ cup (90 g) of Cheddar cheese.

Meanwhile, in a small saucepan over medium-low heat, warm the chili. (Alternatively, you can warm the chili in the microwave.)

Spoon the chili over each burger and top each serving with more Cheddar cheese and the red onion.

MAKES: 4 SERVINGS

1 lb (450 g) ground beef

2 tsp (4 g) dried minced onion

2 tsp (10 ml) Worcestershire sauce

2 tsp (6 g) Montreal steak seasoning

1 lb (450 g) frozen French fries

1½ cups (180 g) shredded Cheddar cheese, plus more as needed, divided

1 (10-oz [280-g]) can hot dog chili

½ small red onion, finely chopped

CORN DOG MUFFINS

These Corn Dog Muffins make the perfect picky eater–friendly lunch or dinner. Sliced hot dogs are baked in corn muffins for a fun twist on a corn dog.

In a medium bowl, whisk together the corn muffin mix, eggs and milk.

Spray 12 silicone cupcake liners with the spray oil. Divide the corn bread batter among the 12 liners.

Add a few hot dog slices to each muffin.

Place six muffins in the air fryer basket and air-fry them at 320°F (160°C) for 12 minutes. Repeat this process with the remaining corn muffins.

Serve the corn dog muffins with the ketchup and mustard.

MAKES:
4 SERVINGS

2 (9-oz [255-g]) boxes corn muffin mix

2 large eggs

$2/3$ cup (160 ml) milk

Spray oil

4 hot dogs, thickly sliced

Ketchup, to serve

Mustard, to serve

TATER TOT CASSEROLE

Tater Tot Casserole doesn't sound fancy because, well, it's not. But it is delicious, it is filling and it does come together super fast when you have a hungry family waiting for dinner to get to the table.

In a medium skillet over medium heat, cook the beef for 8 to 10 minutes, breaking it apart as it cooks, until it is browned. Drain off the grease. Turn off the heat and stir in the mushroom soup, Worcestershire sauce, garlic salt, black pepper and onion powder and stir to combine.

Transfer the casserole filling to a 1½-quart (1.4-L) baking dish. Top the casserole with the tater tots.

Air-fry the casserole at 350°F (177°C) for 15 minutes. Top the casserole with the Cheddar cheese and air-fry the casserole at 350°F (177°C) for 2 to 3 minutes, until the cheese is melted.

TIP: Add a drained 15-ounce (425-g) can of green beans or corn to the meat mixture before baking.

MAKES:
8 SERVINGS

1 lb (454 g) ground beef

1 (11-oz [312-g]) can cream of mushroom soup

2 tsp (10 ml) Worcestershire sauce

½ tsp garlic salt

½ tsp black pepper

1 tsp onion powder or dried minced onion

1 (1-lb [454-g]) bag frozen tater tots

1 cup (120 g) shredded Cheddar cheese, divided

CHEESY BAKED ZITI

Here's another classic Italian dinner made in half the time, thanks to the air fryer. Tender ziti pasta with a hearty meat sauce and loads of cheese make this a family favorite alongside some garlic bread like my Three-Cheese Garlic Bread (page 200).

In a medium skillet over medium heat, cook the beef for 8 to 10 minutes, breaking it apart as it cooks, until it is browned. Turn off the heat and add the pasta sauce.

While the meat is cooking, bring a large pot of salted water to a boil over high heat. Add the ziti and cook it for about 8 minutes, until it is al dente. Drain the ziti and set it aside.

In a large bowl, mix together the ricotta cheese and 1 cup (112 g) of the mozzarella cheese. Add the ziti and toss it with the cheese mixture to coat.

Spread some of the meat sauce in the bottom of 2 (1½-quart [1.4-L]) baking dishes that fit in the air fryer. Fill each baking dish halfway up with the pasta mixture. Top the pasta with more meat sauce.

Divide the rest of the pasta mixture between the two baking dishes. Top each one with the rest of the meat sauce. Top each with ½ cup (56 g) of the mozzarella.

Cover each baking dish with foil. Place one dish in the air fryer and air-fry the ziti at 360°F (182°C) for 20 minutes. Remove the foil and air-fry the ziti at 360°F (182°C) for 3 minutes, until the cheese has melted. Repeat this process with the other baking dish.

Garnish the ziti with the parsley (if using) prior to serving.

**MAKES:
8 SERVINGS**

1 lb (454 g) ground beef

1 (24-oz [680-ml]) jar pasta sauce

1 lb (454 g) ziti pasta

1 cup (123 g) ricotta cheese

2 cups (224 g) mozzarella cheese, divided

Coarsely chopped fresh parsley (optional)

TIP: Swap out the ground beef for ground Italian sausage.

CRISPY POTATO AND CHEESE PIEROGIES

Pierogies are delicious all on their own, but coat them in bread crumbs and crisp them in the air fryer and you have a delicious meal. I serve them with sour cream for dipping.

Spray the air fryer basket with the spray oil.

Place the eggs in a shallow dish. In a second shallow dish, mix together the bread crumbs, garlic salt, paprika, black pepper and Parmesan cheese.

Dip each pierogi in the egg, then into the bread crumbs.

Place half of the pierogies in the air fryer basket and spray the tops with the spray oil.

Air-fry the pierogies at 400°F (204°C) for 8 minutes, flipping them halfway through the cooking time. Repeat this process with the remaining pierogies.

MAKES:
4 SERVINGS

Spray oil

3 large eggs, beaten

2 cups (240 g) traditional bread crumbs

1½ tsp (5 g) garlic salt

2 tsp (6 g) paprika

½ tsp black pepper

1 tbsp (11 g) grated Parmesan cheese

1 lb (454 g) cheese and potato pierogies

PERFECT PATTY MELT

My grandma and I love a good patty melt, and the air fryer makes them perfectly toasty in just minutes. Toasty bread, Thousand Island dressing, Swiss cheese and caramelized onions come together to make the most delicious patty melt.

In a medium bowl, mix together the beef, dried minced onion and Worcestershire sauce. Divide the beef into four equal portions and shape them into patties.

Place two patties in the air fryer and air-fry them at 375°F (191°C) for 8 minutes, flipping them halfway through the cooking time. Repeat this process with the remaining patties. Set them aside.

In a medium skillet over medium-high heat, melt 1 tablespoon (15 g) of the butter. Add the onion and sauté it for 8 minutes, until it is tender.

Using the remaining 4 tablespoons (60 g) of the butter, butter one side of each slice of bread. Place 2 slices of bread in the air fryer, buttered side down, and build a patty melt: Spread ½ tablespoon (8 ml) of the Thousand Island dressing on each slice of bread. Next, add 1 slice of Swiss cheese to each piece of bread. Add a patty, 1 tablespoon (8 g) of the onion and a second slice of Swiss cheese. Top the Swiss cheese with another slice of bread, buttered side up.

Air-fry the patty melts at 400°F (204°C) for 2 minutes on each side. Repeat this process with the remaining ingredients to make two more patty melts.

Slice each sandwich in half prior to serving.

MAKES: 4 SERVINGS

1 lb (454 g) ground beef

2 tsp (4 g) dried minced onion

2 tsp (10 ml) Worcestershire sauce

5 tbsp (75 g) butter, softened, divided

1 small onion, thinly sliced

8 slices bread

¼ cup (60 ml) Thousand Island dressing

8 slices Swiss cheese

ASIAN BEEF AND BROCCOLI

When we order takeout, beef and broccoli is something I know the whole family will enjoy. But why spend money on takeout when you can make it in your air fryer at home? Tender, flavorful beef and crisp broccoli make the perfect meal with a little steamed rice.

To make the beef and broccoli, dredge the steak in the cornstarch and set aside.

Place the broccoli in the air fryer and air-fry it at 390°F (199°C) for 5 minutes.

Add the steak to the broccoli in the air fryer and air-fry at 390°F (199°C) for 10 minutes, stirring the mixture once or twice during the cooking time.

Meanwhile, make the sauce. In a medium saucepan over medium heat, whisk together the oil, garlic, soy sauce, black pepper, red pepper flakes, ½ cup (120 ml) of the water and brown sugar.

In a small bowl, mix together the cornstarch and the remaining 1 tablespoon (15 ml) of cold water. When the sauce comes to a boil, whisk in the cornstarch slurry. Cook the sauce for 2 to 3 minutes, until it has thickened. Add the beef and broccoli to the sauce.

Serve the beef and broccoli over the rice and garnish with sesame seeds (if using).

MAKES:
4 SERVINGS

Beef and Broccoli

1 lb (454 g) flank or skirt steak, thinly sliced

¼ cup (36 g) cornstarch

4 cups (700 g) frozen broccoli florets

4 cups (640 g) cooked white rice

Sesame seeds (optional)

Sauce

2 tsp (10 ml) oil of choice

3 cloves garlic, minced

½ cup (120 ml) low-sodium soy sauce

½ tsp black pepper

½ tsp red pepper flakes

½ cup (120 ml) water plus 1 tbsp (15 ml) cold water, divided

¾ cup (108 g) brown sugar

1 tbsp (9 g) cornstarch

MEATLOAF SLIDERS

What is the best part of meatloaf? The leftovers! I love to make a good meatloaf grilled cheese the next day. I decided to skip waiting for leftovers and make these little Meatloaf Sliders. Start with a great meatloaf recipe and melty cheese and you will have a batch of delicious Meatloaf Sliders that everyone will love.

In a large bowl, mix together the beef, Worcestershire sauce, dried minced onion, steak seasoning, garlic salt, black pepper, egg and bread crumbs. Divide the mixture into 12 portions and form them into little patties.

Place six patties in the air fryer and spread some barbecue sauce on top of the patties. Top each one with 1 or 2 slices of the bell pepper.

Air-fry the patties at 400°F (204°C) for 10 to 12 minutes. Top each patty with ½ slice of American cheese. Air-fry the patties at 400°F (204°C) for 1 minute to melt the cheese. Repeat this process with the remaining ingredients to make six more sliders.

Place a patty on each Hawaiian roll and place the top bun on the patty.

TIP: You can top these with ketchup instead of barbecue sauce.

MAKES:
4 SERVINGS

1 lb (450 g) lean ground beef

1 tsp Worcestershire sauce

1 tsp dried minced onion

1 tsp steak seasoning

1 tsp garlic salt

⅛ tsp black pepper

1 large egg, beaten

½ cup (60 g) traditional bread crumbs

4 tbsp (60 ml) barbecue sauce

½ small green bell pepper, thinly sliced

6 slices American cheese, cut in half

12 mini Hawaiian rolls, sliced

HOT HONEY CHICKEN STRIPS

Chicken strips are always a go-to when I need to feed a table of picky eaters—but sometimes I want to spice them up a bit. These Hot Honey Chicken Strips are full of flavor from hot sauce and sweet honey, the perfect balance of sweet and spicy.

Spray the air fryer basket with the spray oil.

In a shallow dish, mix together the flour, garlic salt, black pepper, paprika and cayenne pepper. Place the eggs in a second shallow dish. Place the panko bread crumbs and traditional bread crumbs in a third shallow dish.

Dredge the chicken in the flour mixture, then dip the chicken in the egg, then coat it in the bread crumbs.

Place half of the chicken strips in the air fryer basket and spray them with the spray oil. Air-fry the chicken strips at 400°F (204°C) for 10 minutes, flipping them once during the cooking time. Repeat the process with the remaining chicken strips.

In a small bowl, whisk together the honey and hot sauce. Drizzle the sauce all over the chicken strips.

MAKES:
4 SERVINGS

Spray oil

2 cups (240 g) all-purpose flour

1 tsp garlic salt

1½ tsp (3 g) coarse black pepper

1 tbsp (9 g) paprika

½ tsp cayenne pepper

2 large eggs, beaten

1 cup (55 g) panko bread crumbs

1 cup (120 g) traditional bread crumbs

1 lb (454 g) boneless, skinless chicken tenderloins

1 cup (240 ml) honey

1 tbsp (15 ml) Buffalo hot sauce

CHEDDAR-STUFFED STEAK HOUSE BURGER

Sometimes you just want a big, thick burger with all the toppings. I love making burgers in my air fryer because I don't have to worry about standing over the stove, getting splattered with grease. These burgers are spiced with steak house seasoning, stuffed with plenty of cheese and topped with crisp red onion for a truly magnificent dish.

In a large bowl, mix together the beef, Worcestershire sauce, dried minced onion, black pepper and steak seasoning. Form the mixture into four balls. In the middle of each ball, place a cube of the Cheddar cheese. Cover the cheese with the meat and shape the balls into patties.

Place the patties in the air fryer and air-fry them at 370°F (188°C) for 12 to 15 minutes, flipping the patties halfway through the cooking time.

Top each patty with a slice of Cheddar cheese and air-fry the burgers at 370°F (188°C) for 1 minute.

Place a patty on each brioche bun and top the patty with the onion, lettuce and tomato.

MAKES:
4 SERVINGS

1 lb (454 g) ground beef

2 tsp (10 ml) Worcestershire sauce

2 tsp (4 g) dried minced onion

1 tsp coarse black pepper

2 tsp (6 g) Montreal steak seasoning

4 (1½-inch [4-cm]) cubes Cheddar cheese

4 slices Cheddar cheese

4 brioche buns

Thinly sliced red onion, to serve

Lettuce leaves, to serve

Thickly sliced tomato, to serve

GARLIC-PARMESAN CHICKEN STRIPS

I have made these Garlic-Parmesan Chicken Strips a million times, they are just that good. Flavored with garlic and Parmesan, these chicken strips are great with a side of pasta, on top of a salad or just dipped in my garlic-Parmesan sauce.

Spray the air fryer basket with the spray oil.

In a shallow dish, combine the buttermilk and garlic, then add the chicken strips. In another shallow dish, mix together ½ cup (90 g) of the Parmesan cheese, flour, bread crumbs, garlic salt and 1 teaspoon of the black pepper. Coat each chicken strip in the flour mixture.

Place half of the chicken strips in the air fryer and air-fry them at 380°F (193°C) for 15 minutes, until the chicken's internal temperature reaches 165°F (74°C). Repeat this process with the remaining chicken strips.

To make the dipping sauce, mix together the garlic-Parmesan dressing, remaining 1 teaspoon of black pepper and remaining 2 teaspoons (7 g) of Parmesan cheese.

MAKES:
4 SERVINGS

Spray oil

1 cup (240 ml) buttermilk

3 cloves garlic, smashed

1 lb (454 g) boneless, skinless chicken tenderloins

½ cup (90 g) plus 2 tsp (7 g) grated Parmesan cheese, divided

1 cup (120 g) all-purpose flour

1 cup (120 g) Italian-seasoned bread crumbs

2 tsp (6 g) garlic salt

2 tsp (4 g) black pepper, divided

1 cup (240 ml) garlic-Parmesan dressing

ASIAN MEATBALLS

These Asian Meatballs are a great twist on classic meatballs. Full of aromatic garlic and onion, these meatballs are topped with a sweet garlic sauce and are perfect to serve with fried rice. This quick dinner will have your family cleaning their plates.

In a medium bowl, mix together the beef, bread crumbs, garlic salt, black pepper and 2 tablespoons (12 g) of the green onion. Form the mixture into 1-inch (2.5-cm) meatballs.

Place half of the meatballs in the air fryer and air-fry them at 400°F (204°C) for 11 minutes. Repeat this process with the remaining meatballs.

Meanwhile, in a medium saucepan over medium heat, mix together the soy sauce, vinegar, brown sugar, cola and garlic. In a small bowl, mix together the cornstarch and water. Whisk this slurry into the sauce when it comes to a boil. Cook the sauce for 2 minutes to allow it to thicken.

Add the meatballs to the sauce, serve them over the rice and top with the remaining green onion.

MAKES:
4 SERVINGS

1 lb (454 g) ground beef

½ cup (60 g) traditional bread crumbs

1 tsp garlic salt

1 tsp black pepper

4 tbsp (24 g) diced green onion, divided

¾ cup (180 ml) soy sauce

1 tbsp (15 ml) rice wine vinegar

1 cup (144 g) brown sugar

¾ cup (180 ml) cola

2 cloves garlic, minced

1½ tbsp (14 g) cornstarch

1 tbsp (15 ml) water

Cooked white or brown rice, to serve

CHEESY BEEF AND BEAN TACOS

Another Taco Tuesday favorite, Cheesy Beef and Bean Tacos are full of ground beef, refried beans and cheese and heated to melty, crispy perfection in the air fryer. When they come out, we top them with lettuce, tomato, sour cream and salsa. These are a favorite with everyone.

Spray the air fryer basket with the spray oil.

In a large skillet over medium heat, cook the beef for 8 to 10 minutes, breaking it apart as it cooks, until it is browned. Drain the excess grease. Add the taco seasoning and water and stir to combine. Add the refried beans and green chilis and stir to combine. Remove the skillet from the heat and add the Colby Jack cheese.

Divide the meat among the tortillas. Fold the tortillas over to create tacos.

Place a single layer of tacos in the air fryer and spray them with the spray oil. Place an air fryer rack on top of the tacos to keep them secure during cooking. (Alternatively, you may also secure each taco with a toothpick.)

Air-fry the tacos at 380°F (193°C) for 5 minutes. Repeat this process with the remaining tacos.

Serve the tacos with the lettuce, tomato, sour cream and salsa.

**MAKES:
4 TO 6 SERVINGS**

Spray oil

1 lb (454 g) ground beef

1 (1-oz [28-g]) packet taco seasoning

¼ cup (60 ml) water

1 (16-oz [454-g]) can refried beans

2 tbsp (30 g) canned diced green chilis

2 cups (224 g) shredded Colby Jack cheese

10 to 12 (4½-inch [11-cm]) corn or flour tortillas

Coarsely chopped lettuce, to serve

Diced tomato, to serve

Sour cream, to serve

Salsa, to serve

QUESO CHICKEN AND FRIES

This recipe is a nod to my favorite order at my local Mexican restaurant. I spice chicken with garlic and cumin and mix it with caramelized onions. Next, I air-fry French fries until they are golden. The chicken and onions go on top of the fries and the whole thing is smothered in queso. So delicious!

In a small bowl, mix together the garlic salt, black pepper, onion powder, paprika, cumin and oil. Rub the spice mixture over all of the chicken breasts.

Place the chicken breasts in the air fryer and air-fry them at 360°F (182°C) for 18 minutes, flipping them once during the cooking time, until their internal temperature reaches 165°F (74°C). Remove the chicken from the air fryer.

Place the French fries in the air fryer and air-fry them at 380°F (193°C) for 12 to 15 minutes, shaking the air fryer basket once or twice during the cooking time.

Meanwhile, thickly slice the chicken. Warm up the queso in a small saucepan over low heat.

Arrange the chicken over the fries and top everything with the queso.

MAKES:
4 SERVINGS

2 tsp (6 g) garlic salt

1 tsp black pepper

2 tsp (6 g) onion powder

1 tsp paprika

2 tsp (6 g) ground cumin

2 tbsp (30 ml) oil of choice

4 (4-oz [113-g]) boneless, skinless chicken breasts

1 lb (454 g) frozen French fries

1 (15-oz [425-ml]) jar white queso dip

SWEET AND SOUR CHICKEN

This is another take-out favorite you can make quickly in your own kitchen thanks to the air fryer. Sweet and Sour Chicken is popular in my house when we order delivery, but now I skip the takeout and make this right at home.

Spritz the air fryer basket with the spray oil. In a large bowl, mix together the garlic salt and cornstarch. Add the chicken and toss to coat the pieces in the mixture.

Place all of the chicken, onion, red bell pepper, green bell pepper and pineapple in the air fryer.

Spray the chicken, vegetables and pineapple with the spray oil and air-fry the mixture at 400°F (204°C) for 12 minutes, flipping the mixture once during the cooking time.

Meanwhile, make the sauce. In a small saucepan over medium-high heat, mix together ¼ cup (60 ml) of the reserved the pineapple juice, vinegar, ketchup, soy sauce and brown sugar. Bring the sauce to a bubble and allow it to cook for 2 minutes.

Toss the chicken and veggies with the sauce and serve them over the rice.

MAKES:
4 SERVINGS

Spray oil

¼ tsp garlic salt

2 tsp (6 g) cornstarch

1 lb (454 g) boneless, skinless chicken thighs, cut into bite-sized pieces

1 small onion, cut into bite-sized pieces

1 small red bell pepper, cut into bite-sized pieces

1 small green bell pepper, cut into bite-sized pieces

1 (10-oz [283-g]) can pineapple chunks, drained and juice reserved

¼ cup (60 ml) distilled white vinegar

¼ cup (68 g) ketchup

2 tbsp (30 ml) low-sodium soy sauce

2 tbsp (18 g) brown sugar

4 cups (640 g) cooked white or brown rice, to serve

BROCCOLI AND CHEDDAR—STUFFED CHICKEN

This comforting dinner stuffs chicken breasts with broccoli and Cheddar. These come out flavorful and moist every time. This is one of those quick dinners I know everyone in my house will eat.

Place a parchment round in the air fryer basket and spritz it with the spray oil.

Cut a deep pocket in each of the chicken breasts.

In a large bowl, mix together the broccoli, Cheddar cheese and cream cheese until the ingredients are combined. Stuff a quarter of the broccoli mixture in each chicken breast.

In a small bowl, mix together the oil, paprika, garlic salt and black pepper. Rub the spice mixture on each chicken breast.

Place the chicken breasts in the air fryer.

Air-fry the chicken breasts at 360°F (182°C) for 20 to 25 minutes, until their internal temperature reaches 165°F (74°C).

TIP: You can secure the chicken breasts closed with toothpicks if you like.

MAKES:
4 SERVINGS

Spray oil

4 (4-oz [113-g]) boneless, skinless chicken breasts

1½ cups (263 g) broccoli florets, finely chopped

1½ cups (180 g) thickly shredded sharp Cheddar cheese

4 oz (113 g) garlic-herb cream cheese, softened

1 tbsp (15 ml) oil of choice

1 tsp paprika

1 tsp garlic salt

1 tsp black pepper

TOASTED MEATBALL SUBS

Toasted Meatball Subs are such a family-friendly dinner—this recipe is one of my boys' favorites. I cook my meatballs in the air fryer before piling them on soft buns with marinara and plenty of cheese. I toast them in the air fryer to melt the cheese and get the buns nice and warm.

In a large bowl, mix together the beef, bread crumbs, egg, Parmesan cheese, 1½ teaspoons (5 g) of garlic salt and Italian seasoning. Divide the mixture into 12 to 16 portions and roll them into meatballs.

Air-fry the meatballs at 400°F (204°C) for 8 to 10 minutes.

In a small bowl, combine the butter with the remaining 1 teaspoon of garlic salt and brush the garlic butter on the insides of the sub buns. Place three to four meatballs in each sub bun. Spoon ¼ cup (60 ml) of the marinara sauce on top of the meatballs. Top each sub with 2 slices of the provolone cheese.

Air-fry the subs at 400°F (204°C) for 1 to 2 minutes to melt the cheese. Sprinkle the subs with the parsley (if using).

MAKES:
4 SERVINGS

1 lb (454 g) ground beef

¼ cup (30 g) traditional bread crumbs

1 large egg

¼ cup (45 g) grated Parmesan cheese

2½ tsp (8 g) garlic salt, divided

½ tsp Italian seasoning

2 tbsp (30 g) butter, melted

4 sub buns

1 cup (240 ml) marinara sauce

8 slices provolone cheese

Coarsely chopped fresh parsley (optional)

CRISPY BEEF LUMPIA

My whole family loves lumpia. It is such a treat to have, but we don't have it that often because of all the frying (which no one wants to do). But with my air fryer, I can get fresh and crispy lumpia whenever I want without all the frying mess.

Spray the air fryer basket with the spray oil.

Place the beef in a large bowl.

In a food processor, combine the carrot, celery, green onions, garlic, soy sauce, garlic salt and black pepper. Add the veggie mixture and the egg to the beef and stir to combine.

Place about 2 tablespoons (30 g) of the filling on a lumpia wrapper and tuck in the ends and roll it all the way up, being sure to seal the edge with water. Repeat this process until you run out of the lumpia filling.

Place the lumpia in the air fryer basket in a single layer. Spray the lumpia with the spray oil.

Air-fry the lumpia at 400°F (204°C) for 16 minutes, flipping them once during the cooking process. Repeat this process with the remaining lumpia.

Serve the lumpia with the sweet chili sauce.

TIP: The meat mixture can be made a day ahead of time; it gets better as it sits. You can also freeze the uncooked lumpia to cook later—just add 2 to 4 minutes to the cooking time.

MAKES:
4 TO 6 SERVINGS

Spray oil

1 lb (454 g) lean ground beef

1 small carrot, coarsely chopped

1 small rib celery, coarsely chopped

6 green onions, coarsely chopped

2 cloves garlic

1 tbsp (15 ml) low-sodium soy sauce

1 tsp garlic salt

½ tsp black pepper

1 large egg, beaten

20 to 24 lumpia wrappers

Sweet chili sauce or duck sauce, to serve

BUFFALO CHICKEN TAQUITOS

Whenever I have some leftover chicken, I make these Buffalo Chicken Taquitos for lunch. Spicy chicken and cream cheese rolled up in a crunchy tortilla make a taquito that is perfect for dipping in ranch.

Spray the air fryer basket with the spray oil.

In a medium bowl, mix together the cream cheese, Colby Jack cheese and hot sauce. Stir in the chicken.

Lay out the tortillas on a work surface and evenly divide the chicken mixture among them. Roll up all the tortillas.

Place six of the taquitos in a single layer in the air fryer basket. Spray the taquitos with the spray oil and sprinkle them with a little kosher salt.

Air-fry the taquitos at 375°F (191°C) for 8 minutes, flipping them halfway through the cooking time. Repeat this process with the remaining six taquitos.

Serve the taquitos with the ranch dressing.

TIP: You can also use corn tortillas for these!

MAKES:
12 TAQUITOS

Spray oil

8 oz (227 g) cream cheese, softened

½ cup (56 g) shredded Colby Jack cheese

½ cup (120 ml) Buffalo hot sauce

3 cups (375 g) shredded cooked chicken

12 (6-inch [15-cm]) flour tortillas

Kosher salt

Ranch dressing, to serve

CHICKEN-FRIED STEAK STRIPS WITH WHITE GRAVY

Is there anything more comforting or heartier than chicken-fried steak? I like to make it in the air fryer and use steak strips that are perfect for dunking in white gravy. Serve my Chicken-Fried Steak Strips with White Gravy with a side of mashed potatoes and you will be in comfort food heaven.

To make the steak, spray the air fryer basket with the spray oil.

In a shallow dish, mix together the flour, paprika, garlic salt, black pepper, onion powder and seasoned salt. In a second shallow dish, mix together the eggs and milk.

Place the panko bread crumbs in a third shallow dish.

Coat each steak strip in the flour mixture, then in the egg mixture and then in the panko bread crumbs.

Lay half of the strips in the air fryer basket in a single layer. Spray the strips with the spray oil.

Air-fry the steak strips at 360°F (182°C) for 12 to 15 minutes, flipping them once during the cooking time. Repeat this process with the remaining strips.

While the steak strips are air-frying, make the white gravy. In a small saucepan over medium heat, melt the butter. Whisk in the flour, salt and black pepper. Cook the mixture for about 2 minutes, until it is slightly browned. Slowly whisk in the milk and bring the mixture to a bubble. Whisk the gravy for 2 to 3 minutes, until it has thickened.

Serve the steak strips with the white gravy for dipping.

MAKES: 4 SERVINGS

Steak
Spray oil

1 cup (120 g) all-purpose flour

1 tsp paprika

1 tsp garlic salt

½ tsp black pepper

½ tsp onion powder

½ tsp seasoned salt

2 large eggs

½ cup (120 ml) milk

2 cups (110 g) panko bread crumbs

1½ lbs (680 g) cube steak, cut into 1-inch (2.5-cm) thick strips

White Gravy
¼ cup (60 g) butter

¼ cup (30 g) all-purpose flour

½ tsp salt

½ tsp coarse black pepper

2 cups (480 ml) milk

MEXICAN LASAGNA

Mexican Lasagna is a spin-off of a classic lasagna. Taco-seasoned beef, refried beans and green chili–studded ricotta cheese make this Mexican Lasagna out of this world. Your family will be asking for this every week.

In a medium skillet over medium heat, cook the beef for 8 to 10 minutes, breaking it apart as it cooks, until it is browned. Drain any excess grease. Add the enchilada sauce to the beef.

In a medium bowl, mix together the ricotta cheese and green chilis.

In each of two 8-inch (20-cm) baking pans that fit in the air fryer, start to build the lasagna.

Spread about one third of the meat sauce among the two baking pans. Lay down 1 tortilla. Spread some refried beans on each tortilla. Add a little of the ricotta mixture to each one. Add a layer of the meat sauce, followed by a layer of the Colby Jack cheese. Top the cheese with another tortilla. Repeat this process two more times.

Cover the baking pans with foil and air-fry the lasagnas, one at a time, at 325°F (163°C) for 40 minutes.

TIP: Serve this with all of your favorite taco toppings.

MAKES:
6 SERVINGS

1 lb (454 g) ground beef

1 (10-oz [283-ml]) can red enchilada sauce

2 cups (246 g) ricotta cheese

1 (4-oz [113-g]) can diced green chilis, drained

8 (8-inch [20-cm]) flour tortillas

2 cups (480 g) refried beans

2½ cups (280 g) shredded Colby Jack cheese

CRISPY POTATO BURRITO

When I got a crispy potato taco from the drive-through, I became obsessed. Now I make them at home but in a big burrito. I get the potatoes crunchy in the air fryer, then roll them up with a spicy sauce, lettuce and cheese. So good and so easy.

In a large bowl, mix together the oil and taco seasoning. Toss the potatoes in the seasoned oil until they are well coated.

Place all of the potatoes in the air fryer and air-fry them at 380°F (193°C) for 12 to 15 minutes, shaking the basket occasionally, until the potatoes are crisp.

Meanwhile, mix together the sour cream and adobo sauce in a small bowl. Set the sauce aside.

On each tortilla, spread some of the sour cream–adobo sauce. Next, place a quarter of the potatoes on each tortilla. Top the potatoes with the Colby Jack cheese, lettuce and green onion. Roll the burrito and enjoy.

MAKES:
4 SERVINGS

1 tbsp (15 ml) oil of choice

1 tbsp (9 g) taco seasoning

1 lb (454 g) baby potatoes, quartered

¼ cup (30 g) sour cream

2 tbsp (30 ml) adobo sauce from chipotles in adobo

4 (10-inch [25-cm]) tortillas

1 cup (112 g) shredded Colby Jack cheese

Shredded lettuce, to serve

2 tbsp (12 g) coarsely chopped green onion, to serve

FIRECRACKER CHICKEN CRESCENTS

Firecracker chicken is a dinner my family asks for a lot, but it can be time-consuming. So I use my air fryer to make these Firecracker Chicken Crescents. Sweet and spicy chicken tenderloins get rolled up in buttery crescent rolls for a quick version of a family favorite. These are seriously good. Your family will thank you.

In a small bowl, mix together the brown sugar and Buffalo sauce.

Place all of the chicken tenderloins in a small baking dish that fits in the air fryer. (Try to arrange the chicken in a single layer; some overlap is okay.) Pour the sauce over the chicken.

Air-fry the chicken at 370°F (188°C) for 12 minutes.

Remove the chicken from the air fryer and let it cool slightly. Wrap each chicken tenderloin in a triangle of the crescent roll dough.

Place a parchment round in the air fryer basket and spritz it with the spray oil. Place a single layer of the crescents in the air fryer. (You may need to work in batches.)

Air-fry the crescents at 320°F (160°C) for 6 to 8 minutes, until the crescent rolls are golden.

**MAKES:
4 SERVINGS**

1 cup (144 g) brown sugar

⅓ cup (80 ml) Buffalo sauce

8 boneless, skinless chicken tenderloins

1 (8-oz [227-g]) can crescent rolls

Spray oil

CHICKEN GYROS

My husband loves gyros, and I use my air fryer to make perfectly spiced, moist chicken to go on pillowy flatbread with all the fixings. It has become a favorite around my house, and I know you will love it too.

Yogurt Sauce

2 cups (570 g) plain Greek yogurt

1 small cucumber, peeled, seeded and grated

1½ tsp (2 g) dried dill

2 cloves garlic, minced

1 tsp distilled white vinegar

1 tsp fresh lemon juice

1 tbsp (15 ml) extra virgin olive oil

1 tsp salt

1 tsp coarse black pepper

MAKES:
4 SERVINGS

Chicken Gyros

4 cloves garlic, minced

2 tbsp (30 ml) fresh lemon juice

2 tsp (10 ml) red wine vinegar

2 tbsp (30 ml) oil of choice

1 tbsp (3 g) dried oregano

1 tsp black pepper

1 lb (454 g) boneless, skinless chicken breasts

4 pita breads

Lettuce leaves, to serve

1 small tomato, thinly sliced, to serve

1 small red onion, thinly sliced, to serve

To make the yogurt sauce, combine the yogurt, cucumber, dill, garlic, distilled white vinegar, lemon juice, olive oil, salt and black pepper in a medium bowl. Set the sauce aside in the refrigerator.

To make the chicken gyros, combine the garlic, lemon juice, red wine vinegar, oil, oregano and black pepper in a large bowl. Add the chicken to the marinade and marinate it for 1 hour.

Air-fry the chicken breasts at 360°F (182°C) for 18 minutes, flipping them once during the cooking time, until their internal temperature reaches 165°F (74°C). Remove the chicken breasts from the air fryer and let them rest for 10 minutes before slicing them thinly.

Stuff each pita with a quarter of the chicken. Add the lettuce, tomato and onion. Drizzle the gyros with the yogurt sauce.

COMPANY'S COMING

Did you know you could make guest-worthy meals in the air fryer? You may think you can only throw together snacks and warm up fries in the air fryer, but you will be amazed at all the gorgeous meals you can make. Impress your guests and make entertaining easy by using your air fryer to whip up delicious recipes like Chicken Cordon Bleu (page 397), Caramelized Honey Ham (page 442) and Lemon-Roasted Cornish Hens (page 417). These recipes are made to impress, be delicious and get you in and out of the kitchen quickly so you can spend more time with your company and less time cooking.

APPLE CIDER–GLAZED HAM STEAK

This simple ham steak gets taken to the next level when it is brushed with an amazing apple cider glaze. This Apple Cider–Glazed Ham Steak evokes all of those fall feelings with its sweet apple cider glaze.

In a small saucepan over medium-high heat, whisk together the brown sugar, mustard and apple cider. Bring the mixture to a bubble and simmer for 10 to 15 minutes, or until the glaze has thickened and reduced.

Place the ham steak in the air fryer basket and brush on some of the apple cider glaze.

Air-fry the ham steak at 400°F (204°C) for 10 to 12 minutes.

MAKES:
4 SERVINGS

¼ cup (36 g) brown sugar

2 tbsp (30 g) Dijon mustard

1 cup (240 ml) apple cider

1 (1-lb [454-g]) ham steak

CHICKEN CORDON BLEU

Chicken cordon bleu always sounds so fancy, and people probably assume it is a difficult dish to make. It is so easy. Impress your guests and serve this crispy chicken stuffed with ham and Swiss cheese. It goes perfectly with Cheesy Garlic Potato Au Gratin (page 207).

Lay a parchment round in the air fryer basket and spray it with the spray oil.

Slice a pocket in the side of each chicken breast and stuff 2 slices of Swiss cheese and 2 slices of ham in each pocket.

Place the flour in a shallow dish. In a second shallow dish, whisk together the eggs and mustard. In a third shallow dish, mix together the panko bread crumbs, black pepper and Parmesan cheese.

Dredge each chicken breast in the flour, followed by the egg mixture, followed by the bread crumb mixture.

Place the chicken breasts in the air fryer basket and spray them with the spray oil.

Air-fry the chicken breasts at 350°F (177°C) for 9 minutes. Flip the chicken breasts and air-fry them at 350°F (177°C) for another 9 minutes, until their internal temperature reaches 165°F (74°C).

MAKES: 4 SERVINGS

Spray oil

4 (4-oz [113-g]) boneless, skinless chicken breasts

8 slices Swiss cheese

8 slices deli ham

½ cup (60 g) all-purpose flour

2 large eggs, beaten

2 tbsp (30 g) Dijon mustard

2 cups (110 g) cup panko bread crumbs

1 tsp black pepper

⅓ cup (60 g) grated Parmesan cheese

HERB-ROASTED TURKEY LEGS

Turkey isn't just for Thanksgiving! I grew up eating turkey legs all year. They are inexpensive and delicious. Deliciously seasoned and roasted in the air fryer, these Herb-Roasted Turkey Legs are perfect for entertaining.

In a small bowl, mix together the sage, thyme, black pepper, garlic salt, onion powder and paprika.

Brush the turkey legs with the butter and rub each leg with the seasoning mix.

Place the turkey legs in the air fryer in a single layer and air-fry them at 400°F (204°C) for 20 minutes. Flip the turkey legs and air-fry them at 400°F (204°C) for another 20 minutes.

MAKES:
4 SERVINGS

2 tsp (2 g) ground sage

1½ tsp (2 g) ground thyme

½ tsp black pepper

1 tsp garlic salt

1 tsp onion powder

1 tsp paprika

4 turkey legs

4 tbsp (60 g) butter, melted and cooled

RANCH ROAST BEEF WITH POTATOES

I love to have guests over for a nice roast beef dinner, and the air fryer gets this amazing Ranch Roast Beef with Potatoes done in half the time the oven would. Ranch-seasoned roast beef is cooked to perfection alongside crispy potatoes. It is an exquisite meal.

**MAKES:
4 TO 6 SERVINGS**

1 (4-lb [1.8-kg]) top round roast beef

2 tbsp (30 ml) oil of choice, divided

2 tsp (6 g) garlic salt, divided

1 tsp black pepper, divided

2 tbsp (18 g) ranch dressing mix, divided

1 lb (454 g) baby potatoes, halved

Rub the beef with 1 tablespoon (15 ml) of the oil. In a small bowl, mix together 1 teaspoon of the garlic salt, ½ teaspoon of the black pepper and 1 tablespoon (9 g) of the ranch dressing mix.

Rub the seasoning mix all over the beef and place it in the air fryer basket. Air-fry the beef at 360°F (182°C) for 20 minutes.

Meanwhile, in a large bowl, toss the potatoes with the remaining 1 tablespoon (15 ml) of oil, remaining 1 teaspoon of garlic salt, remaining ½ teaspoon of black pepper and remaining 1 tablespoon (9 g) of ranch dressing mix.

Flip the roast and add the potatoes to the air fryer basket around the roast. Air-fry the roast and potatoes at 360°F (182°C) for 20 minutes. Flip the roast and stir the potatoes halfway through the cooking time. The beef's internal temperature should reach about 145°F (63°C).

Remove the roast from the air fryer and set it aside to rest.

Air-fry the potatoes at 400°F (204°C) for 5 to 8 minutes, until they are crispy.

Slice the roast beef and serve it with the potatoes.

TIP: You can add some carrots with the potatoes for another layer of flavor.

CHEESE-FILLED ITALIAN MEATBALLS

Everyone loves Italian food, so it is a great choice when you have company coming. These Cheese-Filled Italian Meatballs are wonderful on top of a pile of spaghetti. They are always a guest favorite.

In a large bowl, combine the Italian sausage, beef, garlic salt, onion powder, egg, bread crumbs and Parmesan cheese. Form the mixture into 16 portions.

Make an indent in each portion of the meatball mixture and place 1 cube of mozzarella cheese in the indentation.

Cover the cheese completely with the meat mixture and roll the mixture into meatballs.

Place all of the meatballs in the air fryer and air-fry them at 400°F (204°C) for 12 minutes.

Meanwhile, in a saucepan over medium heat, warm the marinara sauce.

Add the cooked meatballs to the sauce.

TIP: I like to serve these with pasta, but you can eat them as they are alongside a salad or use them in subs!

MAKES: 4 SERVINGS

8 oz (227 g) ground Italian sausage

8 oz (227 g) ground beef

1 tsp garlic salt

1 tsp onion powder

1 large egg

⅓ cup (40 g) traditional bread crumbs

¼ cup (45 g) grated Parmesan cheese

16 (1-inch [2.5-cm]) cubes fresh mozzarella cheese

2 cups (480 ml) marinara sauce

CAJUN CHICKEN AND SHRIMP ALFREDO

Chicken Alfredo is a classic and wonderful dish. But I decided to jazz it up and add shrimp and Cajun seasonings, taking the same old Alfredo and turning it into a dish fabulously full of flavor.

In a small bowl, mix together the Cajun seasoning, garlic salt and black pepper.

In a large bowl, mix together the chicken, ½ tablespoon (8 ml) of the oil and half of the seasoning mixture. Toss the chicken until it is well coated.

Place all of the chicken in the air fryer and air-fry it at 400°F (204°C) for 10 minutes.

Meanwhile, in another large bowl, toss the shrimp with the remaining ½ tablespoon (8 ml) of oil and the remaining seasoning mixture.

Bring a large pot of salted water to a boil over high heat. Add the fettuccine noodles and cook them for 8 to 10 minutes, until they are al dente. Drain the fettuccine.

In a medium saucepan over medium heat, warm the Alfredo sauce.

Add the shrimp to the chicken in the air fryer and air-fry them at 400°F (204°C) for 3 to 5 minutes, until the shrimp are pink.

Combine the fettuccine with the Alfredo sauce and place the pasta on a platter. Pile the chicken and shrimp on top of the fettuccine.

MAKES:
4 SERVINGS

2½ tsp (8 g) Cajun seasoning

1 tsp garlic salt

½ tsp black pepper

8 oz (227 g) boneless, skinless chicken tenderloins, cut into bite-sized pieces

1 tbsp (15 ml) oil of choice, divided

1 lb (454 g) large raw shrimp, peeled and deveined

1 lb (454 g) fettuccine noodles

2 cups (480 ml) Alfredo sauce

MINI CHILI TAMALE PIES

Serving these Mini Chili Tamale Pies in little ramekins is so fun. I fill the ramekins with a delicious chili and top it with a cheesy corn bread. I love making these for guests, especially when it starts to get chilly outside.

In a large skillet over medium heat, combine the beef, onion and garlic. Cook the mixture for 8 to 10 minutes, breaking the beef apart as it cooks, until it is browned.

Drain off any grease.

Add the chili beans, green chilis, chili powder, cumin, garlic salt and black pepper. Stir to combine the ingredients and remove the skillet from the heat.

In a medium bowl, whisk together the corn muffin mix, egg and milk until they are well combined.

Divide the chili mixture among four ramekins. Top each ramekin with the corn muffin mix.

Place all four ramekins in the air fryer and air-fry the tamale pies at 320°F (160°C) for 12 minutes.

Serve the tamale pies hot, topped with the sour cream and green onion.

**MAKES:
4 SERVINGS**

8 oz (227 g) ground beef

½ small onion, diced

2 cloves garlic, minced

1 (16-oz [454-g]) can chili beans in chili sauce

2 tbsp (30 g) canned diced green chilis, drained

2 tsp (6 g) chili powder

1 tsp ground cumin

½ tsp garlic salt

½ tsp black pepper

1 (9-oz [255-g]) box corn muffin mix

1 large egg

⅓ cup (80 ml) milk

Sour cream, to serve

Coarsely chopped green onion, to serve

GARLIC-BUTTER SHRIMP AND ASPARAGUS FOIL PACKETS

These Garlic-Butter Shrimp and Asparagus Foil Packets are a fun and easy dinner for guests. I prep these ahead of time, then I pop them into the air fryer when the guests arrive and—just like that—dinner is done.

Lay out four 8-inch (20-cm) pieces of foil on a work surface. On each piece of foil, place a quarter of the asparagus. Place a quarter of the shrimp on top of the asparagus.

In a small bowl, mix together the butter, garlic, parsley, garlic salt and black pepper.

Pour the garlic-butter over each packet evenly and fold the foil in the center, rolling it down and then folding up the ends.

Place the packets in the air fryer and air-fry them at 400°F (204°C) for 7 to 9 minutes.

TIP: You can add slices of lemon to your packets before cooking to add a pop of fresh flavor.

MAKES: 4 SERVINGS

1 lb (454 g) asparagus, thick ends snapped off

1½ lbs (680 g) large raw shrimp, peeled and deveined

4 tbsp (60 g) butter, melted

4 cloves garlic, minced

2 tbsp (6 g) finely chopped fresh parsley

1 tsp garlic salt

1 tsp black pepper

CHICKEN MILANESE

Chicken Milanese is an elegant-looking dinner, but it could not be simpler to make. Chicken breasts are pounded thin, breaded and air-fried until they are crispy. I top them with a mixed green salad, and it is gorgeous.

Spray the air fryer basket with the spray oil.

Place the chicken breasts between two sheets of parchment paper and pound them until they are half their original thickness.

In a shallow bowl, whisk together the flour, garlic salt, paprika and black pepper. Place the eggs in a second shallow dish. In a third shallow dish, mix together the bread crumbs and grated Parmesan cheese.

Dredge each chicken breast in the flour mixture, then in the eggs and finally in the bread crumb mixture.

Place 1 or 2 of the chicken breasts in the air fryer basket. Spray the tops with the spray oil. Air-fry the chicken at 400°F (204°C) for 8 minutes, flipping them halfway through the cooking time. Repeat this process with the remaining chicken breasts.

Place each chicken breast on a plate. Pile the baby greens on top of the chicken, then sprinkle the shaved Parmesan cheese over the greens. Squeeze fresh lemon juice over everything.

MAKES:
4 SERVINGS

Spray oil

4 (4-oz [113-g]) boneless, skinless chicken breasts

1 cup (120 g) all-purpose flour

2 tsp (6 g) garlic salt

1 tsp paprika

1 tsp black pepper

3 large eggs, beaten

1 cup (120 g) Italian-seasoned bread crumbs

¼ cup (45 g) grated Parmesan cheese

2 cups (60 g) mixed baby greens

½ cup (90 g) shaved Parmesan cheese

1 small lemon, cut into wedges

RANCH CHICKEN POT PIES

Ranch Chicken Pot Pies are another crowd-pleasing meal all your guests will rave over. A rich chicken filling topped with flaky dough will be a favorite with all of your guests, and you'll love how fast it comes together.

In a large bowl, mix together the chicken, ranch dressing mix, cream of chicken soup, milk, black pepper and mixed vegetables.

Divide the filling among four ramekins.

Roll out the crescent roll dough into a rectangle and cut out circles that fit the tops of the ramekins. Place the dough on each pot pie and cut a slit in the middle of the dough. Brush the tops of the pot pies with the butter.

Air-fry the pot pies at 320°F (160°C) for 10 to 12 minutes.

MAKES: 4 SERVINGS

2 cups (250 g) shredded cooked chicken

1½ tbsp (14 g) ranch dressing mix

1 (11-oz [312-ml]) can cream of chicken or cream of celery soup

¼ cup (60 ml) milk

½ tsp black pepper

1 (15-oz [425-g]) can mixed vegetables, drained

1 (8-oz [227-g]) can crescent rolls

2 tbsp (30 g) butter, melted

BARBECUE–CRANBERRY CHICKEN THIGHS

Chicken thighs are such a great choice when entertaining. They are inexpensive but full of flavor and so tender. I love brushing them with this barbecue-cranberry sauce for a quick but delightful dinner when I have guests.

Air-fry the chicken thighs at 375°F (191°C) for 9 minutes.

Meanwhile, in a medium bowl, whisk together the cranberry sauce, barbecue sauce and brown sugar.

Brush the sauce on the chicken thighs and air-fry them at 400°F (191°C) for 9 minutes. Brush the thighs with sauce again and serve.

MAKES:
4 SERVINGS

8 bone-in chicken thighs

1 cup (100 g) canned cranberry sauce

1 cup (240 ml) barbecue sauce

2 tbsp (18 g) brown sugar

LEMON–ROASTED CORNISH HENS

Cornish hens always look elegant and appetizing. They are handy when you have guests, as you can make succulent roasted chicken in no time. Their smaller size makes them perfect for the air fryer. These Lemon-Roasted Cornish Hens are flavorful and delicious!

In a small bowl, combine the butter, garlic salt, black pepper, paprika and lemon juice.

Place a lemon half in the cavity of each hen.

Brush the butter mixture all over the hens. If your air fryer is big enough, place both hens in the air fryer, breast side down, and air-fry them at 400°F (204°C) for 10 minutes. Flip the hens and air-fry them at 400°F (204°C) for 10 minutes, until their internal temperature reaches 165°F (74°C).

Let the hens rest for 10 minutes.

MAKES: 2 SERVINGS

2 tbsp (30 g) butter, melted

1 tsp garlic salt

1 tsp black pepper

1 tsp paprika

Juice of 1 small lemon

1 small lemon, halved

2 (1- to 2-lb [454- to 908-g]) Cornish hens

COCONUT-LIME SHRIMP

Shrimp is always a favorite when entertaining. I like to coat my shrimp in shredded coconut for extra crunch. These are coated in a lime-infused coconut milk before they get their coconut breading, which gives them an additional layer of flavor. Serve these with extra lime wedges for squeezing over top.

Spray the air fryer basket with the spray oil.

In a shallow dish, mix together the flour, black pepper and paprika. Place the eggs in a second shallow dish. In a third shallow dish, mix together the coconut and panko bread crumbs.

Dredge each shrimp in the flour mixture, then in the eggs, then in the coconut-panko mixture.

Place a single layer of shrimp in the air fryer basket and spray the shrimp with the spray oil. Air-fry the shrimp at 400°F (204°C) for 3 minutes. Flip the shrimp and air-fry them at 400°F (204°C) for 5 minutes. Repeat this process with the remaining shrimp.

In a small bowl, mix together the honey, lime juice and lime zest. Drizzle the sauce over the shrimp.

Serve the shrimp with the lime wedges.

MAKES: 4 SERVINGS

Spray oil

1 cup (120 g) all-purpose flour

1 tsp black pepper

1 tsp paprika

2 large eggs, beaten

2 cups (150 g) unsweetened flaked coconut

1 cup (55 g) panko bread crumbs

1 lb (454 g) large raw tail-on shrimp, peeled and deveined

½ cup (120 ml) honey

½ cup (120 ml) fresh lime juice

1 tbsp (6 g) lime zest

Lime wedges, to serve

BACON-WRAPPED PORK LOIN

Bacon-Wrapped Pork Loin always makes an impression when served for dinner. This is one of my favorite dinners, and it goes well with mashed potatoes and Brussels sprouts.

On a work surface, lay out the strips of bacon in a row. Lay the pork tenderloin on the bacon and roll it up in the strips of bacon.

In a small bowl, mix together the brown sugar and mustard.

Brush the brown sugar mixture all over the pork and place it in the air fryer basket.

Air-fry the pork at 360°F (182°C) for 25 minutes.

Let the pork rest for 5 minutes, then slice it.

MAKES:
4 SERVINGS

4 to 5 strips bacon

1 (2- to 3-lb [908-g to 1.4-kg]) pork tenderloin

⅓ cup (48 g) brown sugar

1 tbsp (15 g) Dijon mustard

COUNTRY-STYLE BARBECUE RIBS

I love to entertain in the summer, and ribs are always high on my list for dinner. But I don't always feel like standing over a hot grill, or sometimes the weather doesn't behave. That is when I turn to my air fryer to make these spectacular Country-Style Barbecue Ribs.

Spray the air fryer basket with the spray oil.

In a small bowl, mix together the garlic salt, paprika and black pepper. Rub the seasoning on the ribs.

Air-fry the ribs at 400°F (204°C) for 5 minutes.

Baste the ribs with the barbecue sauce. Air-fry the ribs at 400°F (204°C) for 5 minutes.

Flip the ribs and baste them with more barbecue sauce. Air-fry them at 400°F (204°C) for 10 minutes.

**MAKES:
4 SERVINGS**

Spray oil

1 tsp garlic salt

1 tsp paprika

1 tsp black pepper

1 lb (454 g) boneless country pork ribs

1 cup (240 ml) barbecue sauce

CORNMEAL–CRUSTED CRISPY FISH TACOS

Cornmeal-Crusted Crispy Fish Tacos are so gorgeous, so light, so fresh. How could you not want to eat a dozen of these? I love making these in the summer for friends, but they also bring a bit of sunshine and summer flavor to even the coldest days.

Spray the air fryer basket with the spray oil.

Slice each tilapia fillet to make two 'strips.

In a shallow dish, mix together the cornmeal, paprika, cumin, garlic salt and black pepper. Fill a second shallow dish with water. Dip the fish in the water, then in the cornmeal mixture.

Lay the fish in the air fryer in a single layer and spray it with spray oil. (You may need to work in batches.)

Air-fry the fish at 400°F (204°C) for 13 to 14 minutes, flipping it halfway through the cooking time.

In a medium bowl, combine the mayonnaise, honey and lime juice. Add the cabbage and toss to coat it in the dressing.

Place some fish on each tortilla and top it with some of the cabbage slaw and avocado slices. Serve the tacos with the lime wedges.

TIP: You can use any firm white fish for these tacos.

MAKES: 4 SERVINGS

Spray oil
1 lb (454 g) tilapia fillets
1½ cups (255 g) cornmeal
1½ tsp (5 g) paprika
1½ tsp (5 g) ground cumin
1½ tsp (5 g) garlic salt
1 tsp black pepper
Water
½ cup (110 g) mayonnaise
2 tbsp (30 ml) honey
Juice of 1 small lime
1½ cups (510 g) thinly sliced red cabbage
8 (6- to 8-inch [15- to 20-cm]) tortillas
Avocado slices
Lime wedges, to serve

THE BEST MARINATED STEAK
WITH MUSHROOMS

Everyone needs a good steak recipe under their belt, and this is mine. Perfectly seasoned and cooked to medium-rare in the air fryer, this steak is where it is at! Served with roasted mushrooms on top, this steak is fit for a king. Or a queen. Or anyone, really.

MAKES:
4 SERVINGS

To make the steak, whisk together the soy sauce, oil, Worcestershire sauce, garlic, black pepper and steak seasoning in a small bowl. Transfer the marinade to a gallon (3.8-L) ziplock bag and add the steaks. Marinate the steaks for 30 minutes.

Meanwhile, prepare the mushrooms. Gently wipe the mushrooms with a damp cloth.

In a medium bowl, combine the oil, garlic salt and black pepper. Add the mushrooms and toss to coat them in the oil mixture.

Air-fry the mushrooms at 380°F (193°C) for 12 minutes.

Remove the mushrooms from the air fryer and set them aside.

Place the steaks in the air fryer and air-fry them at 400°F (204°C) for 10 to 12 minutes, flipping them once during the cooking time.

Let the steaks rest for 10 minutes, then serve them with the mushrooms.

Marinated Steak

2 tbsp (30 ml) low-sodium soy sauce

2 tbsp (30 ml) oil of choice

2 tbsp (30 ml) Worcestershire sauce

2 cloves garlic, minced

1 tsp black pepper

2 tsp (6 g) Montreal steak seasoning

4 (4- to 6-oz [113- to 170-g]) rib eye or petite sirloin steaks

Mushrooms

1 lb (454 g) white button mushrooms

2 tbsp (30 ml) oil of choice

1 tsp garlic salt

½ tsp black pepper

FIRECRACKER SHRIMP

Firecracker Shrimp is hands down my mom's favorite meal. These sweet and spicy shrimp are mouthwatering. I serve this on rice to make sure we get every last drop of that amazing firecracker sauce.

Lay a parchment round in the air fryer basket and spray it with the spray oil.

In a medium bowl, whisk together the brown sugar, hot sauce and vinegar.

Dip each shrimp in the sauce and lay it in the air fryer.

Air-fry the shrimp at 400°F (204°C) for 4 minutes. Flip the shrimp and baste the other side with the sauce. Air-fry the shrimp at 400°F (204°C) for 4 more minutes.

Serve the shrimp over the rice.

MAKES:
4 SERVINGS

Spray oil

1 cup (144 g) light brown sugar

¼ cup (60 ml) thick Buffalo hot sauce

1 tbsp (15 ml) apple cider vinegar

2 lbs (908 g) large raw shrimp, peeled and deveined

Cooked white or brown rice, to serve

RODEO MEATLOAF WITH ONION RINGS

I was reminded the other day of a cheeseburger sold by a certain fast food place that has barbecue sauce, cheese and onion rings on it. I thought to myself, "That would make a great meatloaf." Of course, I don't have time to wait for meatloaf to cook when I have hungry kids—so I make mini meatloaves in my air fryer, which come out juicy and delicious. And that crispy, caramelized meatloaf top everyone fights over? Everyone gets their own with this recipe.

MAKES:
4 SERVINGS

In a medium bowl, mix together the beef, Worcestershire sauce, dried minced onion, steak seasoning, garlic salt, black pepper, egg and bread crumbs together until the ingredients are well combined. Form the mixture into four oval patties.

Place the meatloaves in the air fryer basket and air-fry them at 350°F (177°C) for 15 minutes.

Top each meatloaf with 1 tablespoon (15 ml) of the barbecue sauce. Air-fry the meatloaves at 350°F (177°C) for 5 minutes.

Top each meatloaf with 1 tablespoon (8 g) of the Cheddar cheese. Air-fry the meatloaves at 350°F (177°C) for 1 minute.

Remove the meatloaves from the air fryer and set them aside to rest.

Meanwhile, air-fry the onion rings at 400°F (204°C) for 6 to 0 minutes. Top the meatloaves with the onion rings.

1 lb (454 g) lean ground beef

1 tsp Worcestershire sauce

1 tsp dried minced onion

1 tsp steak seasoning

1 tsp garlic salt

⅛ tsp black pepper

1 large egg, beaten

½ cup (60 g) traditional bread crumbs

4 tbsp (60 ml) barbecue sauce

4 tbsp (32 g) shredded Cheddar cheese

4 frozen onion rings

TIP: You can use Cheddar slices to make these extra cheesy! And feel free to air-fry more onion rings to serve on the side.

DEVILED CRAB CAKES

My mom and I love crabs. My mom used to make deviled crab all the time, and it was my favorite. I decided to turn that yummy deviled crab into these Deviled Crab Cakes, and they are a winner! These crab cakes are full of crab and little filler but bursting with flavor. Serve these with a salad and you will have an impressive dinner for your guests.

Place a parchment round in the air fryer basket and spray it with the spray oil.

In a large bowl, mix together the green onions, mayonnaise, mustard, lemon juice, Worcestershire sauce and Old Bay Seasoning. Add the crabmeat and bread crumbs and stir to combine the ingredients.

Form the crab mixture into four crab cakes.

Place the crab cakes in the air fryer basket and spritz the tops with the spray oil. Sprinkle them with the paprika.

Air-fry the crab cakes at 400°F (204°C) for 6 to 8 minutes.

MAKES: 4 SERVINGS

Spray oil

2 green onions, finely chopped

2 tbsp (28 g) mayonnaise

1 tbsp (15 g) yellow mustard

2 tsp (10 ml) fresh lemon juice

2 tsp (10 ml) Worcestershire sauce

1 tsp Old Bay Seasoning

8 oz (227 g) lump crabmeat

2 tbsp (16 g) traditional bread crumbs

Paprika

CRISPY GARLIC CHICKEN BREASTS

Is there anything better than a juicy chicken breast with perfectly crispy skin? I love making these Crispy Garlic Chicken Breasts in my air fryer because they come out flawless every time: juicy, tender white meat with flavorful, crispy skin. These are great to serve to guests or for a quick weeknight dinner.

In a small bowl, combine the butter, garlic salt, dried minced onion, black pepper, paprika and garlic.

Brush each chicken breast with the butter-garlic mixture.

Place the chicken breasts in the air fryer and air-fry them at 370°F (188°C) for 30 minutes, until the chicken's internal temperature reaches 165°F (74°C). (You may need to work in batches.)

MAKES: 4 SERVINGS

4 tbsp (60 g) butter, melted

2 tsp (6 g) garlic salt

2 tsp (4 g) dried minced onion

1 tsp black pepper

1 tsp paprika

2 cloves garlic, minced

4 (6- to 8-oz [170- to 227-g]) bone-in, skin-on split chicken breasts

KOREAN BEEF WONTONS

These Korean Beef Wontons might impress your guests, but you and I know they come together in no time! Korean-spiced ground beef, carrots and cabbage are tucked into crispy wonton wrappers, making a spectacular dish to serve your guests.

Spray the air fryer basket with the spray oil.

In a large skillet over medium heat, cook the beef for 8 to 10 minutes, breaking it apart as it cooks, until it is browned. Drain any excess grease and return the skillet to medium heat. Add the cabbage and carrots. Cook the mixture for 5 to 10 minutes, until the cabbage begins to soften.

Add the brown sugar, soy sauce, garlic, ginger, red pepper flakes and green onion. Cook the mixture for 5 minutes.

On a work surface, lay out the wonton wrappers and place about 2 teaspoons (10 g) of the filling on each wonton wrapper. Fold the wrapper over to make a triangle, sealing the edges with a little water.

Lay a single layer of wontons in the air fryer basket and spray the tops with the spray oil.

Air-fry the wontons at 350°F (177°C) for 8 minutes, flipping them halfway through the cooking time. Repeat the process with the remaining wontons.

MAKES:
4 TO 6 SERVINGS

Spray oil

1 lb (454 g) lean ground beef

½ cup (170 g) shredded cabbage

½ cup (25 g) grated carrots

½ cup (72 g) brown sugar

¼ cup (60 ml) low-sodium soy sauce

3 cloves garlic, minced

¼ tsp ground ginger

½ tsp red pepper flakes

2 tbsp (12 g) coarsely chopped green onion

20 wonton wrappers

HONEY-PECAN CHICKEN THIGHS

How good do these Honey-Pecan Chicken Thighs sound? I'll tell you: Tender chicken thighs are cooked in the air fryer until the skin gets crispy and crunchy. Then they're drizzled with a honey-pecan glaze. This is one meal you will be making again and again.

In a small bowl, whisk together the brown sugar, honey, mustard and pecans.

Sprinkle the chicken thighs with the salt and black pepper. Air-fry the chicken thighs at 400°F (204°C) for 5 minutes.

Baste the chicken thighs with the honey-pecan glaze and air-fry them at 400°F (204°C) for 8 minutes. Baste them again and air-fry them at 400°F (204°C) for another 5 minutes.

MAKES:
4 SERVINGS

½ cup (72 g) brown sugar

3 tbsp (45 ml) honey

1 tbsp (15 g) Dijon mustard

½ cup (60 g) coarsely chopped pecans

8 skin-on, bone-in chicken thighs

2 tsp (10 g) salt

1 tsp black pepper

STUFFED PORK CHOPS

WITH CRANBERRY GLAZE

I love making these Stuffed Pork Chops with Cranberry Glaze for friends. All of my favorite holiday flavors are packed into these pork chops. They are especially pretty garnished with dried cranberries and parsley.

Cut a slit in the side of each pork chop to create a pocket for the stuffing.

In a medium saucepan over high heat, bring the water and butter to a boil. Remove the saucepan from the heat and stir in the stuffing with a fork.

In a medium bowl, whisk together the cranberry sauce, brown sugar and mustard.

Fill the pork chops with the stuffing and place them in the air fryer basket. Brush each pork chop with the cranberry sauce mixture. Air-fry the pork chops at 390°F (199°C) for 12 minutes.

MAKES:
4 SERVINGS

4 (¾- to 1-inch [19-mm to 2.5-cm]-thick) pork chops

1½ cups (360 ml) water

4 tbsp (60 g) butter

1 (6-oz [170-g]) box corn bread stuffing

1 cup (280 g) canned cranberry sauce

1 tbsp (9 g) brown sugar

1 tbsp (15 g) Dijon mustard

CARAMELIZED HONEY HAM

Honey ham is one of my weaknesses, and I love the holidays because we always have honey ham. I discovered I could make amazing Caramelized Honey Ham in the air fryer. No more waiting for the holidays to get my ham fix—now I can make this delicious sweet ham anytime I have a craving. I love using presliced boneless hams. They fit right in my air fryer and are delicious.

Line an 8-inch (20-cm) round baking pan with foil. Place the ham in the prepared baking pan.

In a small bowl, whisk together the brown sugar, pineapple juice and honey. Pour half of the honey mixture over the ham and cover the baking pan with foil. Place the pan in the air fryer and air-fry the ham at 375°F (191°C) for 20 minutes.

Remove the ham from the air fryer basket and remove the top layer of foil. Place the ham back in the pan uncovered. Brush the ham with the honey mixture. Air-fry the ham at 400°F (204°C) for 5 minutes. Baste the ham with the honey mixture again and air-fry the ham at 400°F (204°C) for 5 minutes. Baste the ham one last time and air-fry it at 400°F (204°C) for 5 minutes.

MAKES:
8 SERVINGS

1 (3-lb [1.4-kg]) cooked presliced boneless ham

½ cup (72 g) brown sugar

3 tbsp (45 ml) pineapple juice

¼ cup (60 ml) honey

SESAME SALMON

This Sesame Salmon is going to be your new go-to recipe when you have guests. Salmon is always a good choice when you have guests because it cooks so quickly. This salmon is a little sweet and a little garlicky, and I use two different colors of sesame seeds to really make it special. It looks fabulous and tastes just as great!

In a small bowl, whisk together the honey, soy sauce, garlic, sesame oil, white sesame seeds, black sesame seeds and cayenne pepper.

Place the salmon in an 8-inch (20-cm) round baking pan and pour the sauce all over the salmon.

Place the pan in the air fryer and air-fry the salmon at 400°F (204°C) for 8 to 10 minutes.

Serve the salmon over the rice or with the steamed vegetables (if using).

MAKES:
4 SERVINGS

⅓ cup (80 ml) honey

3 tbsp (45 ml) low-sodium soy sauce

3 garlic cloves, minced

2 tsp (10 ml) sesame oil

½ tbsp (5 g) white sesame seeds

½ tbsp (5 g) black sesame seeds

¼ tsp cayenne pepper

4 (1- to 2-inch [2.5- to 5-cm] -thick) skin-on salmon fillets

Cooked white or brown rice, to serve (optional)

Steamed vegetables, to serve (optional)

INSIDE-OUT CHICKEN PARMESAN

Inside-Out Chicken Parmesan is a fantastic recipe. Chicken is stuffed with plenty of mozzarella and marinara and lightly breaded before being cooked to perfection in the air fryer. Served on a bed of pasta, this one is sure to wow your guests.

Spray the air fryer basket with the spray oil.

Cut a deep pocket in the side of each chicken breast, being careful not to cut all the way through the chicken.

Fill each pocket with ¼ cup (60 ml) of the marinara sauce and 2 slices of the mozzarella cheese.

In a shallow dish, mix together the flour, garlic salt, onion powder, Italian seasoning and black pepper. Place the eggs in a second shallow dish. In a third shallow dish, combine the panko bread crumbs and Parmesan cheese.

Gently dredge each chicken breast in the flour, then in the eggs, then in the panko mixture. Place the chicken breasts in the air fryer and spray the tops with the spray oil.

Air-fry the chicken at 350°F (177°C) for 20 minutes. Serve the chicken over spaghetti and garnish with the shaved Parmesan and parsley (if using).

MAKES:
4 SERVINGS

Spray oil

4 (4-oz [113-g]) boneless, skinless chicken breasts

1 cup (240 ml) marinara sauce

8 slices fresh mozzarella cheese

1 cup (120 g) all-purpose flour

1 tsp garlic salt

1 tsp onion powder

1 tsp Italian seasoning

1 tsp black pepper

2 large eggs, beaten

2 cups (110 g) panko bread crumbs

½ cup (90 g) grated Parmesan cheese

1 lb (454 g) cooked spaghetti (optional)

Shaved Parmesan cheese (optional)

Finely chopped parsley (optional)

CHEESY MASHED POTATO HASSELBACK CHICKEN

This chicken is a showstopper for sure. I cut the chicken Hasselback-style and season it with garlic salt and paprika. In addition, this chicken has little pockets of cheesy mashed potatoes. If you are looking to make something a little different than the usual chicken for your guests, try this Cheesy Mashed Potato Hasselback Chicken.

Bring a large pot of salted water to a boil over high heat. Add the potatoes. Boil the potatoes until they are fork-tender, about 15 minutes. Drain the potatoes and place the potatoes back in the hot pot. Add the milk, butter, 1 cup (120 g) of the Cheddar cheese, salt and black pepper.

Mash the potatoes with a potato masher until they are smooth or still a little chunky, according to your preference.

Cut four to six slits across the top of each chicken breast, being sure not to cut all the way through.

In a small bowl, mix together the oil, garlic salt and paprika. Rub the oil mixture on all of the chicken breasts.

Fill each slit in the chicken with the mashed potatoes.

Place the chicken breasts in the air fryer and air-fry them at 350°F (177°C) for 20 minutes.

Sprinkle the remaining 1 cup (120 g) of Cheddar cheese on the chicken breasts. Air-fry the chicken at 350°F (177°C) for 1 minute to melt the cheese.

MAKES: 4 SERVINGS

4 medium russet potatoes, peeled and cut into bite-sized chunks

½ cup (120 ml) milk

3 tbsp (45 g) butter

2 cups (240 g) sharp Cheddar cheese, divided

1 tsp salt

½ tsp black pepper

4 (4-oz [113-g]) boneless, skinless chicken breasts

1 tbsp (15 ml) oil of choice

1 tsp garlic salt

1 tsp paprika

MINI MEXICAN PIZZAS

Mexican pizzas are a weakness of mine at a certain drive-through. I like to make a big platter of these mini ones to serve to guests. They take no time to make and are always a big hit.

Spray the air fryer basket with the spray oil.

In a medium skillet over medium heat, cook the beef for 8 to 10 minutes, breaking it apart as it cooks, until it is browned. Drain any excess grease. Add the water and taco seasoning, stirring to combine the ingredients.

On a work surface, lay out 8 mini tortillas and spread refried beans on each one. Top the tortillas with the taco meat.

Place a second tortilla on the top of every pizza.

Place two to four pizzas in the air fryer and spray the tops with the spray oil. Air-fry the pizzas at 400°F (204°C) for 5 minutes. Top the pizzas with the taco sauce and Colby Jack cheese. Air-fry the pizzas at 400°F (204°C) for 2 minutes, until the cheese is melted. Repeat this process with the remaining pizzas.

Top each pizza with the tomato and green onion.

MAKES:
4 SERVINGS

Spray oil

1 lb (454 g) ground beef

¼ cup (60 ml) water

1 (1-oz [28-g]) packet taco seasoning

16 (4½-inch [11-cm]) flour tortillas

1 (16-oz [454-g]) can refried beans

1 cup (240 ml) taco sauce

2 cups (224 g) shredded Colby Jack cheese

1 small tomato, diced

2 tbsp (12 g) coarsely chopped green onion

TIP: Feel free to top these with your favorite toppings, such as sour cream, jalapeños or guacamole.

THE BEST EVER STEAK AND POTATO KEBABS

I really like entertaining with kebab dishes. Something about kebabs just screams party. These Best Ever Steak and Potato Kebabs are marinated in a luscious marinade and skewered with veggies. Your guests are going to love grabbing these off the platter.

In a large bowl, mix together the Russian dressing, soy sauce, honey and black pepper.

Toss the steak pieces with the marinade. Add the potatoes and onion. Marinate the steak and vegetables for 1 hour.

Using metal skewers, skewer the steak, potatoes and onion in an alternating pattern until all of the ingredients are gone.

Place the kebabs in the air fryer in a single layer. Air-fry them at 400°F (204°C) for 10 to 12 minutes, flipping them halfway through the cooking time. Repeat this process with the remaining kebabs.

TIP: These are great with other veggies too. Add your favorite veggies to the marinade and skewer them along with the meat.

MAKES: 4 SERVINGS

1 cup (240 ml) Russian or French dressing

¼ cup (60 ml) soy sauce

¼ cup (60 ml) honey

1 tsp coarse black pepper

4 (4- to 6-oz [113- to 170-g]) petite sirloin steaks, cut into bite-sized pieces

2 (15-oz [425-g]) cans whole potatoes, drained and cut in half if large

1 small red onion, quartered

PARMESAN-PEPPERCORN CHICKEN SANDWICH

This sandwich makes my heart and taste buds sing! This Parmesan-Peppercorn Chicken Sandwich is great to serve guests, but I make it often just for myself. The chicken gets juicy in the air fryer and is topped with bacon and Swiss, but a Parmesan-peppercorn dressing is what really gives this sandwich its awesome flavor.

Spray the air fryer basket with the spray oil.

Place the chicken breasts in the air fryer basket and spray them with the spray oil. Sprinkle the chicken breasts evenly with the garlic salt, paprika and ½ teaspoon of black pepper. Air-fry the chicken at 400°F (204°C) for 8 minutes.

Meanwhile, mix together the Parmesan dressing, Parmesan cheese and remaining ½ tablespoon (3 g) of black pepper in a small bowl.

Top each chicken breast with 1 slice of Swiss cheese.

Spread the Parmesan-peppercorn dressing on the bottom half of each brioche bun. Add a chicken breast to each one and top the chicken with 2 slices of bacon.

Spread a little more dressing on the top bun. Add lettuce and tomato (if using).

TIP: If you can't find Parmesan dressing, you can substitute it with ranch.

MAKES: 4 SERVINGS

Spray oil

4 thin boneless, skinless chicken breasts

2 tsp (6 g) garlic salt

1 tsp paprika

½ tbsp (3 g) plus ½ tsp black pepper, divided

1 cup (240 ml) Parmesan dressing

2 tbsp (22 g) grated Parmesan cheese

4 slices Swiss cheese

4 brioche buns

8 slices cooked bacon

Lettuce leaves, to serve (optional)

Thinly sliced tomato, to serve (optional)

CHICKEN CAESAR CRESCENTS

Chicken Caesar salad used to be the salad to serve. I put a little twist on that by putting marinated chicken, melty cheese and Caesar dressing in a Parmesan-dusted crescent and serving it with a little Caesar salad on the side. These are addicting!

In a gallon (3.8-L) ziplock bag, combine the chicken, Italian dressing and garlic. Marinate the chicken for 1 hour.

Spray the air fryer basket with the spray oil and add the chicken. Air-fry the chicken at 400°F (204°C) for 8 to 10 minutes, until the chicken's internal temperature is 165°F (74°C).

Measure ¼ cup (60 ml) of the Caesar dressing in a small measuring cup. Separate the crescent roll dough into triangles and spread each triangle with a little of the Caesar dressing.

Place a piece of string cheese on each crescent. Add 1 chicken tenderloin and roll up the crescent dough.

Place a parchment round in the air fryer and spritz it with the spray oil.

Place four of the crescents in the air fryer and brush them with the butter. Sprinkle each one with a little grated Parmesan cheese. Air-fry the crescents at 320°F (160°C) for 6 minutes. Repeat this process with the remaining crescents.

Meanwhile, in a large bowl, toss together the romaine, remaining 1 cup (240 ml) of Caesar dressing, croutons and shaved Parmesan cheese.

Serve the crescents alongside the Caesar salad.

MAKES: 4 SERVINGS

8 boneless, skinless chicken tenderloins

1 cup (240 ml) Italian dressing

2 garlic cloves, minced

Spray oil

1¼ cups (300 ml) Caesar dressing, divided

1 (8-oz [227-g]) can crescent rolls

2 sticks mozzarella string cheese, each cut lengthwise into 4 pieces

2 tbsp (30 g) butter, melted

2 tbsp (22 g) grated Parmesan cheese

4 cups (300 g) coarsely chopped romaine lettuce

1 cup (40 g) croutons

Shaved Parmesan cheese

HONEY NUT—CRUSTED CHICKEN TENDERS

Of course chicken tenders can be fancy enough to serve to guests. These Honey Nut–Crusted Chicken Tenders get their crunch from cereal. These are perfect for dipping in honey mustard.

Spray the air fryer basket with the spray oil.

In a shallow dish, mix together the flour and salt. In a second shallow dish, mix together the honey mustard dressing and egg. Place the cereal in a third shallow dish.

Dip the chicken tenderloins in the flour, then in the egg mixture, then in the cereal.

Add half of the chicken tenderloins to the air fryer and spray them with the spray oil. Air-fry the chicken at 400°F (204°C) for 8 minutes, flipping the chicken halfway through the cooking time. Repeat the process with the remaining chicken tenderloins.

Serve the chicken tenders with additional honey mustard dressing for dipping.

MAKES:
4 SERVINGS

Spray oil

1 cup (120 g) all-purpose flour

½ tsp salt

½ cup (120 ml) honey mustard dressing, plus more to serve

1 large egg, beaten

3 cups (225 g) honey nut cereal, crushed

1 lb (454 g) boneless, skinless chicken tenderloins

TURKEY STUFFING MEATBALLS WITH CRANBERRY DIPPING SAUCE

These little Turkey Stuffing Meatballs are moist, full of flavor and use just a few ingredients. They take mere minutes in the air fryer and go great with my Cranberry Dipping Sauce. They're like your favorite parts of a turkey dinner, all rolled up into one.

Spray the air fryer basket with the spray oil.

In a large bowl, mix together the stuffing and chicken stock. Add the turkey, egg, salt and pepper and mix to combine.

Shape the turkey mixture into 1½-inch (4-cm) meatballs.

Place half of the meatballs in the air fryer basket. Air-fry the meatballs at 400°F (204°C) for 8 minutes, flipping them halfway through the cooking time. Repeat the process with the remaining meatballs.

In a small bowl, mix together the cranberry sauce, brown sugar and mustard.

Serve the meatballs with the cranberry sauce for dipping.

MAKES: 4 SERVINGS

Spray oil

1 cup (40 g) boxed corn bread stuffing

½ cup (120 ml) chicken stock

1 lb (454 g) ground turkey

1 large egg

1 tsp salt

1 tsp black pepper

1 cup (280 g) canned cranberry sauce

1 tbsp (9 g) brown sugar

1 tbsp (15 g) Dijon mustard

SWEETS AND TREATS

We have seen how the air fryer creates amazing meals, but did you know it also creates some fabulous desserts? I love that anytime I am craving something sweet or the kids are begging for an after-dinner treat, I can whip something up in just minutes. Everything from cookies to pound cake and even cheesecake bakes up perfectly in the air fryer and in half the time. I'll show you how to make tasty desserts like Banana Bread Pudding (page 503), Molten Lemon Cakes (page 468) and even Mini Churros with Caramel (page 491)—all delicious, all quick, all easy!

BUTTERSCOTCH APPLE TURNOVERS

These pretty little Butterscotch Apple Turnovers are delicious with a scoop of vanilla ice cream. Filled with spiced apples and butterscotch chips and baked right in the air fryer, these make the perfect dessert. I even sneak one for breakfast every now and then—shhh!

Spray the air fryer basket with the spray oil.

In a medium skillet over medium heat, combine the apples, butter, brown sugar and cinnamon. Cook the apples for about 10 minutes, until they are tender.

Lightly roll out the pie crusts into a rectangle shape and cut squares out of each piece of dough, so that you end up with eight equal-sized squares.

Place 1 tablespoon (15 g) of the apple filling in the middle of each square. Top the apples with about 1 tablespoon (11 g) of the butterscotch chips.

Using your finger, moisten the edges of the dough with a little water. Fold the dough over to create a triangle.

Use a fork to crimp the edges of the turnovers. Cut a slit in the middle of each turnover.

In a small bowl, combine the egg and water to create an egg wash. Brush the egg wash on each turnover.

Place four turnovers at a time in the air fryer basket. Air-fry them at 350°F (177°C) for 10 minutes. Repeat this process with the remaining turnovers.

Serve the turnovers hot, at room temperature or cold.

TIP: You can serve these with a scoop of vanilla ice cream and butterscotch sauce. Yum!

MAKES: 8 TURNOVERS

Spray oil

3 medium apples (any variety), thinly sliced

1 tbsp (15 g) butter

1 tbsp (9 g) brown sugar

1 tsp ground cinnamon

2 (9-inch [23-cm]) refrigerated roll-out pie crusts

½ cup (90 g) butterscotch chips

1 large egg, beaten

1 tbsp (15 ml) water

SNICKERDOODLE BLONDIES

Blondies are underrated. I love them, and these Snickerdoodle Blondies have to be my favorite. Vanilla blondies are topped with cinnamon and sugar for a warm, comforting dessert.

Spray a 7-inch (18-cm) cake pan with the spray oil.

In a large bowl, use a hand mixer to whip the butter, 1 cup (192 g) of the granulated sugar and brown sugar for 2 to 3 minutes, until the mixture is light and fluffy. Add the eggs, one at a time, and the vanilla and beat until the ingredients are combined.

In another large bowl, whisk together the flour, 1 teaspoon of the cinnamon, baking powder and salt.

Add the flour mixture to the butter mixture, stirring with a spoon until they are just combined.

Gently stir in the white chocolate chips. Pour the batter into the prepared cake pan.

Air-fry the blondies at 330°F (166°C) for 15 to 18 minutes. The middle should be slightly soft.

Meanwhile, in a small bowl, combine the remaining 2 tablespoons (24 g) of granulated sugar and the remaining 1 teaspoon of cinnamon. Sprinkle the cinnamon sugar all over the top of the blondies and air-fry them at 330°F (166°C) for 2 minutes.

Let the blondies cool before slicing them.

MAKES:
8 TO 12 SERVINGS

Spray oil

¾ cup (180 g) butter, softened

1 cup (192 g) plus 2 tbsp (24 g) granulated sugar, divided

½ cup (72 g) brown sugar

2 large eggs

2 tsp (10 ml) pure vanilla extract

2 cups (240 g) all-purpose flour

2 tsp (6 g) ground cinnamon, divided

¾ tsp baking powder

¼ tsp salt

1 cup (180 g) white chocolate chips

MOLTEN LEMON CAKES

Molten lava cakes will always be popular. Who doesn't love a tender cake with a molten center? Usually these cakes are chocolate, but these Molten Lemon Cakes win my heart, as I am a sucker for anything lemon.

Spray eight ramekins with the spray oil.

In a large microwave-safe bowl, microwave the white chocolate and butter for 30 seconds. Stir the mixture and repeat this process until it is melted and smooth. Whisk in the flour, powdered sugar, lemon curd and vanilla.

Whisk in the eggs and egg yolks until they are well combined.

Divide the batter among the eight ramekins.

Air-fry four of the cakes at 375°F (191°C) for 11 minutes. Do not overbake these. Repeat this process with the remaining four cakes.

Let the cakes cool for 5 minutes.

Gently run a butter knife around the edges of the cakes. Invert the cakes onto plates.

Top the cakes with additional powdered sugar or whipped cream (if using) and serve them immediately.

TIP: These must be served hot to achieve the molten-center effect.

MAKES: 8 CAKES

Spray oil

5 oz (142 g) white chocolate

½ cup (122 g) unsalted butter

⅔ cup (80 g) all-purpose flour

½ cup (65 g) powdered sugar, plus more to serve

½ cup (160 g) jarred lemon curd

1 tsp pure vanilla extract

4 large eggs

4 large egg yolks

Whipped cream, to serve (optional)

S'MORES CHEESECAKE

S'mores Cheesecake gives you all that s'mores flavor you love without all the sticky marshmallow mess. A graham cracker crust and a rich vanilla cheesecake get baked in the air fryer then topped with hot fudge and a toasted marshmallow.

Spritz 18 silicone or foil cupcake liners with the spray oil.

In a medium bowl, mix together the graham cracker crumbs and butter. Press about 1 tablespoon (6 g) of the crust mixture into the bottom of each cupcake liner.

In another large bowl, use a hand mixer to beat the cream cheese and sugar for 2 to 3 minutes, until the mixture is light and fluffy.

Add the eggs, one at a time, then add the sour cream and vanilla and beat until the ingredients are well combined.

Divide the batter evenly among the cupcake liners.

Place half of the cheesecakes in the air fryer and air-fry them at 330°F (166°C) for 5 to 6 minutes. Their centers will still be slightly jiggly. Repeat this process with the remaining cheesecakes.

Refrigerate the cheesecakes for 1 hour.

Once the cheesecakes have chilled, spoon a little of the hot fudge sauce on the top of each one.

Top each cheesecake with a marshmallow and toast the marshmallows using a kitchen torch.

MAKES: 18 CHEESECAKES

Spray oil

1 cup (90 g) crushed graham crackers

3 tbsp (45 ml) melted butter

2 (8-oz [227-g]) blocks cream cheese, softened

2/3 cup (128 g) sugar

2 large eggs

2 tbsp (16 g) sour cream

1 tsp pure vanilla extract

½ cup (120 ml) hot fudge sauce

18 marshmallows

BLUEBERRY HAND PIES

Anytime you need to make a quick dessert, these Blueberry Hand Pies have your back. Pie dough and blueberries bake up into a warm, luscious little pie. Sprinkle them with some powdered sugar and thank me later.

Spray the bottom of the air fryer basket with the spray oil.

Place the blueberries in a medium saucepan. In a small bowl, whisk together the cornstarch and granulated sugar. Pour this mixture over the berries. Add the lemon juice and stir until the ingredients are combined.

Cook the blueberries over medium heat, stirring frequently. Bring the mixture to a simmer and cook it for about 5 minutes to allow it to thicken. Remove the filling from the heat and let it cool.

Meanwhile, lightly roll out the pie crusts and use a 4-inch (10-cm) biscuit cutter to cut 10 circles from each pie crust. Put about 1 tablespoon (15 g) of the blueberry filling in the middle of 10 pieces of dough. Fold the dough circle in half.

Crimp the edges of the pies with a fork and cut a slit in the middle.

In a small bowl, whisk together the egg and water to create an egg wash. Brush the egg wash over the top of each pie and sprinkle a little sanding sugar on top.

Place a single layer of pies in the air fryer. Air-fry the pies at 360°F (182°C) for 6 minutes. Repeat this process with the remaining pies.

Let the pies cool slightly before serving.

MAKES: 10 HAND PIES

Spray oil

2 cups (310 g) frozen blueberries

2½ tbsp (23 g) cornstarch

⅓ cup (64 g) granulated sugar

1 tbsp (15 ml) fresh lemon juice

2 (9-inch [23-cm]) refrigerated roll-out pie crusts

1 large egg, beaten

1 tbsp (15 ml) water

Sanding sugar

PEANUT BUTTER CHEESECAKE BROWNIE CAKE

This is the ultimate brownie recipe: gooey brownies swirled with a peanut butter cheesecake filling. This bakes up fast in the air fryer, so you can get your brownie fix quick.

Note that the best pan for this recipe is a 5 x 5–inch (13 x 13–cm) baking pan or a 6 x 6–inch (15 x 15–cm) baking pan. Both pans should be 3 inches (7.5 cm) deep.

Spray a 5 x 5–inch (13 x 13–cm) or 6 x 6–inch (15 x 15–cm) baking pan that is 3 inches (7.5 cm) deep with the spray oil.

Make the brownie batter according to the directions on the back of the box.

In a medium bowl, use a hand mixer to whip together the cream cheese, peanut butter, egg, flour and sugar.

Pour the brownie batter into the prepared baking pan. Drop dollops of the cream cheese mixture all over the top of the batter.

Run a knife through the cream cheese dollops, dragging the cream cheese mixture through the brownie batter to create a marble effect.

Air-fry the cake at 350°F (177°C) for 25 to 28 minutes, until a toothpick inserted into the center comes out clean (or nearly so). If the cake is not done, air-fry it for 3 to 5 minutes more.

Let the cake cool prior to serving.

MAKES: 8 SERVINGS

Spray oil

1 (18-oz [510-g]) box brownie mix, plus ingredients for brownies listed on box

8 oz (227 g) cream cheese, softened

¼ cup (45 g) peanut butter

1 large egg

1 tbsp (8 g) all-purpose flour

½ cup (96 g) sugar

GIANT LOADED COOKIE

Why waste your time with little cookies when you can have this Giant Loaded Cookie? Packed with goodies like two kinds of chocolate chips, sprinkles, candies and pretzels, this giant cookie is sinful—but a scoop of ice cream on top while it's still warm from the air fryer is heavenly!

Spray a 7-inch (18-cm) round baking pan with the spray oil.

In a large bowl, use a hand mixer to beat together the butter, granulated sugar and brown sugar for 2 to 3 minutes, until the mixture is light and fluffy. Beat in the egg and vanilla until they are combined.

Beat in the baking soda, salt and flour. Gently stir in the mini chocolate chips, white chocolate chips, M&M's and sprinkles.

Pour the batter into the prepared baking pan and top the batter with the pretzels.

Air-fry the cookie at 350°F (177°C) for about 9 minutes. Insert a toothpick into the cookie's center. If the toothpick comes out clean, the cookie is done; if the toothpick does not come out clean, air-fry the cookie for 1 to 2 minutes more.

Serve the cookie topped with the ice cream.

TIP: You can put all sorts of goodies in this cookie, like chocolate chunks, pecans, walnuts, almonds, raisins, dried cranberries, coconut, whatever your family likes!

MAKES:
4 TO 6 SERVINGS

Spray oil

½ cup (120 g) butter, softened

½ cup (96 g) granulated sugar

½ cup (72 g) brown sugar

1 large egg

1 tsp pure vanilla extract

½ tsp baking soda

½ tsp salt

1½ cups (180 g) all-purpose flour

¼ cup (45 g) mini chocolate chips

¼ cup (45 g) white chocolate chips

¼ cup (45 g) mini M&M's

2 tbsp (36 g) sprinkles

¼ cup (30 g) mini pretzels

Ice cream, to serve

PEACH OATMEAL CRUMBLE

This Peach Oatmeal Crumble is like a warm hug. Peach pie filling topped with a crumble of cinnamon-spiced oatmeal—it does not get better than this.

To make the filling, spray four ramekins with the spray oil.

In a large bowl, mix together the peaches, granulated sugar and cinnamon.

Divide the peaches among the prepared ramekins.

To make the topping, mix together the flour, oats, granulated sugar and cinnamon in a medium bowl.

Cut the butter into the flour mixture with a pastry cutter or fork. The mixture should consist of coarse pea-sized crumbs.

Sprinkle the topping all over the peaches.

Air-fry the crumbles at 350°F (177°C) for 15 to 20 minutes.

Serve the crumbles hot with a scoop of the vanilla ice cream and a drizzle of the caramel sauce.

MAKES:
4 SERVINGS

Filling
Spray oil

4 cups (900 g) peeled thickly sliced fresh peaches

1 tbsp (12 g) granulated sugar

1 tsp ground cinnamon

Topping
½ cup (60 g) all-purpose flour

½ cup (40 g) rolled oats

½ cup (96 g) granulated sugar

¼ tsp ground cinnamon

4 tbsp (60 g) butter, cut into slices

Vanilla ice cream, to serve

Caramel sauce, to serve

"FRIED" COOKIE DOUGH BITES

"Fried" cookie dough just sounds dangerous. Don't worry, there will be no deep-frying here. Instead, cookie dough gets wrapped up in flaky dough and baked in the air fryer so it is much healthier for you! Well, as healthy as cookie dough can be.

Line a large baking sheet with parchment paper and set it aside.

In a large bowl, use a hand mixer to beat together the butter, brown sugar and granulated sugar for 2 to 3 minutes, until the mixture is smooth. Add the vanilla and milk and beat until the ingredients are well combined.

Using a wooden spoon, stir in the flour and chocolate chips.

Using a small cookie scoop, form balls of dough and place them on the prepared baking sheet. Freeze the dough balls for 30 minutes.

Unroll the crescent dough from their cans and pinch the seams together. Cut the dough into 3-inch (7.5-cm) squares and place one frozen cookie dough ball in the middle of each square. Cover the cookie dough with the crescent roll dough and roll the parcel into a ball.

Spray the air fryer basket with the spray oil. Place a single layer of cookie dough bites in the air fryer basket, making sure they are not touching.

Spray the cookie dough bites with the spray oil and air-fry them at 350°F (177°C) for 6 minutes. Repeat this process with the remaining cookie dough bites.

Sprinkle the cookie dough bites with the powdered sugar.

MAKES: 8 TO 12 SERVINGS

4 tbsp (60 g) butter, softened

⅓ cup (48 g) light brown sugar

⅓ cup (64 g) granulated sugar

½ tsp pure vanilla extract

¼ cup (60 ml) milk

1 cup (120 g) all-purpose flour

¾ cup (135 g) semisweet chocolate chips

2 (8-oz [227-g]) cans crescent rolls

Spray oil

Powdered sugar, to serve

CHOCOLATE–CHERRY CHEESECAKE BITES

These Chocolate-Cherry Cheesecake Bites are a little taste of heaven. They are the perfect size for a grab-and-go dessert. They are also the perfect size to smuggle out of the fridge for a midnight snack.

Place a silicone or foil cupcake paper liner in 18 muffin pan cavities.

In a large bowl, use a hand mixer to beat the cream cheese, sugar and vanilla until the ingredients are blended together.

Add the eggs, one at a time, mixing on low speed after each addition just until the ingredients are blended together.

Place one chocolate sandwich cookie in the bottom of each cupcake liner. Fill the liners three-quarters full with the cheesecake batter.

Place as many cheesecakes in the air fryer basket as will fit in a single layer. Air-fry the cheesecakes at 320°F (160°C) for 5 to 6 minutes, until the middle is just set.

Place about 1 tablespoon (16 g) of the cherry pie filling on top of each cheesecake. Refrigerate the cheesecakes for 2 hours before serving.

TIP: You can drizzle hot fudge sauce on top of the cheesecakes if you like.

MAKES: 18 CHEESECAKES

3 (8-oz [227-g]) blocks cream cheese, softened

¾ cup (144 g) sugar

1 tsp pure vanilla extract

3 large eggs

18 chocolate sandwich cookies

1 (21-oz [595-g]) can cherry pie filling

MINI CINNAMON PECAN PIES

Toasted pecans are one of my favorite snacks. These cute Mini Cinnamon Pecan Pies cook up in the air fryer, and the pecans get perfectly toasty. I make these in phyllo dough shells, which are light and flaky and are amazing for these little pies.

Place all the pecans in a baking pan that fits in the air fryer. Air-fry them at 350°F (177°C) for 10 minutes, stirring them once or twice during the cooking time.

In a medium bowl, stir together the brown sugar, corn syrup, egg, butter, vanilla and cinnamon.

Divide the pecans among all the phyllo shells and spoon the brown sugar mixture over the top of each one.

Place half of the phyllo shells in the air fryer basket and air-fry the pies at 320°F (160°C) for 10 to 12 minutes. Repeat this process with the remaining pies.

Let the mini pies cool completely before serving.

**MAKES:
15 MINI PIES**

1 cup (120 g) pecans, coarsely chopped

3 tbsp (27 g) brown sugar

3 tbsp (45 ml) dark corn syrup

1 large egg

2 tsp (10 g) butter, melted

½ tsp pure vanilla extract

½ tsp ground cinnamon

15 mini phyllo shells

APPLE PIE CROSTATA

Apple pie from the air fryer? Of course! Apple Pie Crostata to be exact. This crostata has all the flavors of scrumptious apple pie but is so much easier. No need to worry about perfect scalloped edges—this crostata is meant to look rustic.

Lay a parchment round in the air fryer basket and spray it with the spray oil.

In a large bowl, toss together the apples, butter, brown sugar, cinnamon, lemon juice and cornstarch.

Lay the pie crust in the air fryer basket and pour the apple mixture in the center of the pie crust. Fold the edges over all around the crust.

In a small bowl, combine the egg and water to create an egg wash. Brush the edges of the crust with the egg wash and sprinkle it with the sanding sugar.

Air-fry the crostata at 330°F (166°C) for 12 minutes.

Serve the crostata warm.

MAKES:
4 TO 6 SERVINGS

Spray oil

2 medium apples (any variety), thinly sliced

2 tbsp (30 g) butter, melted

2 tbsp (18 g) brown sugar

1 tsp ground cinnamon

1 tsp fresh lemon juice

2 tsp (6 g) cornstarch

1 (9-inch [23-cm]) refrigerated roll-out pie crust

1 large egg, beaten

1 tbsp (15 ml) water

Sanding sugar

CHOCOLATE-ALMOND CROISSANTS

These Chocolate-Almond Croissants are divine. In just a few minutes, you can have a warm croissant filled with melted chocolate and topped with toasted almonds. These are going to be your new favorite thing.

Lay a parchment round in the air fryer basket and spritz it with the spray oil.

Separate the crescent roll dough into eight triangles.

Divide the chocolate chips and almonds among the long ends of the crescents and roll up the dough.

Place four croissants in the air fryer basket and brush them with the butter. Sprinkle a little sanding sugar and more almonds on top of the croissants.

Air-fry the croissants at 320°F (160°C) for 6 minutes. Repeat this process with the remaining croissants.

Serve the croissants warm.

MAKES:
8 SERVINGS

Spray oil

1 (8-oz [224-g]) can crescent rolls

½ cup (90 g) chocolate chips

½ cup (55 g) sliced almonds, plus more as needed

2 tbsp (30 g) butter, melted

Sanding sugar

MINI CHURROS WITH CARAMEL

Who says churros are only for carnivals and Sam's Club? Now you can make these Mini Churros right at home in minutes. Just imagine . . . warm, cinnamon-rich churros fresh out of the air fryer and ready to be dipped into a luscious caramel sauce.

To make the caramel sauce, place the sugar in a medium saucepan over medium-high heat and whisk it while it melts. Cook the sugar for 3 to 5 minutes, until it turns a dark amber color. Whisk in the salt, then add the butter all at once and whisk until it is completely incorporated into the sugar. Remove the saucepan from the heat and pour in the heavy cream. Continue to whisk the mixture for 2 to 3 minutes, until the ingredients form a smooth sauce. Set the sauce aside to cool.

To make the mini churros, combine the water, butter and 1 tablespoon (12 g) of the sugar in a medium saucepan over medium heat. Bring the mixture to a simmer.

Using a wooden spoon, add the flour to the water mixture and quickly stir. Stir the mixture constantly for 2 to 3 minutes, until it is thick. Transfer the flour mixture to a large bowl. Continue to stir until the mixture has cooled slightly. Using a hand mixer, beat in the vanilla and egg. Transfer all the dough to a gallon (3.8-L) ziplock bag and refrigerate it for 1 hour.

Spray the air fryer basket with the spray oil. Preheat the air fryer at 375°F (191°C) for 10 minutes. Snip off the end of the ziplock bag and pipe 2- to 3-inch (5- to 7.5-cm)-long churros right into the air fryer basket. Don't pipe them too close to one another. Spritz the churros with the spray oil. Air-fry them for 10 minutes.

Meanwhile, in a shallow dish, mix together the remaining ½ cup (96 g) of sugar and cinnamon. Remove the churros from the air fryer and transfer them directly to the cinnamon sugar and roll them to coat. Repeat this process until there is no churro batter left.

Serve the churros with the caramel sauce.

MAKES: 12 SERVINGS

Caramel Sauce

1 cup (192 g) sugar

1 tsp fine sea salt

6 tbsp (90 g) unsalted butter, at room temperature

⅔ cup (160 ml) heavy cream, at room temperature

Mini Churros

1 cup (240 ml) water

8 tbsp (120 g) butter, cubed

½ cup (96 g) plus 1 tbsp (12 g) sugar, divided

1 cup (120 g) all-purpose flour

1 tsp pure vanilla extract

1 large egg

Spray oil

1 tsp ground cinnamon

FLUFFERNUTTER BITES

Did you grow up with Fluffernutter sandwiches? Peanut butter and marshmallow creme on white bread is one of my favorite flavor combinations! I wanted to re-create that childhood favorite with these Fluffernutter Bites. Creamy peanut butter and mini marshmallows cook up in crispy wonton wrappers to make the perfect sweet treat.

Spray the air fryer basket with the spray oil.

Place 1 teaspoon of the peanut butter in the middle of a wonton wrapper and top the peanut butter with 4 to 5 mini marshmallows.

Spread water along the edges of each wonton wrapper. Bring together the wrapper's opposite corners and squeeze. Fold up the other two opposite sides and squeeze to seal the Fluffernutter bites.

Place six Fluffernutter bites in the air fryer basket. Spray the tops with the spray oil.

Air-fry the Fluffernutter bites at 380°F (193°C) for 6 minutes. Repeat this process with the remaining six Fluffernutter bites.

Sprinkle the Fluffernutter bites with the powdered sugar (if using).

MAKES:
4 SERVINGS

Spray oil

¼ cup (65 g) creamy peanut butter

12 wonton wrappers

½ cup (25 g) mini marshmallows

Powdered sugar (optional)

CHOCOLATE-HAZELNUT SOUFFLÉ

Though it sounds intimidating, there is no easier dessert than a good soufflé. I love the flavor of hazelnut and chocolate together in this soufflé. A sprinkle of powdered sugar is all that's needed to finish this amazing dessert.

MAKES: 2 SERVINGS

3 oz (85 g) bittersweet chocolate, finely chopped

1 tbsp (19 g) chocolate-hazelnut spread

¼ cup (60 g) butter, plus more as needed

2 large eggs, separated, divided

1 tsp pure vanilla extract

2 tbsp (16 g) all-purpose flour

3 tbsp (36 g) granulated sugar, plus more as needed

Powdered sugar

In a medium microwave-safe bowl, microwave the chocolate, chocolate-hazelnut spread and butter in 30-second intervals until the chocolate is fully melted. Let the mixture cool slightly.

In a large bowl, whisk together the chocolate mixture, egg yolks and vanilla. Fold in the flour until the mixture is smooth and set it aside.

In another large bowl, use a mixer to whip the egg whites for 3 to 5 minutes, until they have soft peaks. Add the sugar, 1 tablespoon (12 g) at a time, with the mixer on high speed for 3 to 5 minutes, until stiff peaks form.

Preheat the air fryer to 330°F (166°C). Meanwhile, grease two ramekins with additional butter. Sprinkle additional sugar into the ramekins, turning to coat the insides.

Dump out the extra sugar from the first ramekin into the other ramekin and repeat.

Gently fold the chocolate mixture into the egg whites. Carefully spoon the batter into each ramekin and place them in the air fryer. Air-fry the soufflés for 13 minutes.

Open the air fryer gently and remove the soufflés. Dust them with the powdered sugar and serve them immediately.

TIP: These are gorgeous served with fresh raspberries on top.

CRANBERRY–WHITE CHOCOLATE OATMEAL COOKIES

I have been making these cookies for years, and I just found out I can make them in the air fryer. Tart dried cranberries go perfectly with the sweet white chocolate chips, and I love the texture from the oatmeal. These are fabulous cookies and are sure to become one of your favorites.

Place a parchment round in air fryer basket and spritz it with the spray oil.

In a large bowl, use a hand mixer to beat together the butter, granulated sugar and brown sugar for 2 to 3 minutes, until the mixture is light and fluffy. Beat in the eggs and vanilla.

In another large bowl, whisk together the oats, flour, powdered pudding, baking soda and salt.

Gradually add the oat mixture to the butter mixture. Gently fold in the white chocolate chips and cranberries.

Using a 1-tablespoon (15-g) cookie scoop, drop the cookie dough onto the prepared parchment, making sure the cookies are about 1 inch (2.5 cm) apart.

Air-fry the cookies at 325°F (163°C) for 8 minutes for a chewy cookie. Place the cookies on a cooling rack to cool while you finish air-frying the rest of the cookies.

MAKES: 6 DOZEN

Spray oil

1 cup (240 g) butter, softened

¾ cup (144 g) granulated sugar

¾ cup (108 g) brown sugar

2 large eggs

1 tsp pure vanilla extract

3 cups (240 g) quick oats

1½ cups (180 g) all-purpose flour

1 (3-oz [85-g]) box instant vanilla pudding

1 tsp baking soda

¼ tsp salt

2 cups (360 g) white chocolate chips

1 cup (120 g) dried cranberries

INDIVIDUAL BUTTER CAKES

Butter cakes are such a simple recipe, but they are so delectable—the perfect little sweet treat. These Individual Butter Cakes don't call for any chocolate or fancy toppings, but they will still blow you away. They bake in just a few minutes. I like to eat mine warm with a simple dollop of whipped cream.

Spray six ramekins with the spray oil.

In a large bowl, use a hand mixer to beat the butter, cream cheese, milk and sugar for 2 to 3 minutes, until the mixture is light and fluffy.

Add the eggs one at a time and continue to mix while adding the vanilla and salt.

Slowly beat the flour into the mixture until the ingredients are just combined.

Fill the prepared ramekins three-quarters full of batter.

Air-fry three or four butter cakes at 350°F (177°C) for 15 minutes, until a toothpick inserted into the center comes out clean. Repeat the process with the remaining butter cakes.

Serve the butter cakes warm with a dollop of the whipped cream on top.

TIP: This cake is great with 1 teaspoon of lemon extract mixed in. You can also serve this with fresh berries.

MAKES:
6 SERVINGS

Spray oil

2 cups (480 g) unsalted butter, softened

3 oz (85 g) cream cheese, softened

2 tbsp (30 ml) milk

2¼ cups (432 g) sugar

2 large eggs

1 tsp pure vanilla extract

½ tsp salt

1½ cups (180 g) all-purpose flour

Whipped cream, to serve

PEAR PIE SLICES

Pear Pie Slices are a different take on pie. Slices of spiced fresh pears are wrapped in pie dough and baked. I drizzle mine with a little caramel.

Place a parchment round in the air fryer basket and spritz it with the spray oil.

In a small bowl, mix together the sugar and cinnamon.

Remove the pie crusts from their packaging and cut each one in half, then cut each half into ½- to 1-inch (13-mm to 2.5-cm) strips.

Brush each pear wedge with the lemon juice. Sprinkle each one with some of the cinnamon sugar.

Wrap one strip of pie crust around each pear wedge.

Brush the pie crust with the butter. Sprinkle a little more cinnamon sugar on each pie slice.

Place half of the pie slices in the air fryer. Air-fry them at 320°F (160°C) for 7 minutes. Repeat this process with the remaining pie slices.

Serve the pie slices warm with the Caramel Sauce for dipping.

MAKES: 12 SLICES

Spray oil

½ cup (96 g) sugar

2 tsp (6 g) ground cinnamon

2 (9-inch [23-cm]) refrigerated roll-out pie crusts

3 large pears (any variety), each cut into 4 wedges

2 tbsp (30 ml) fresh lemon juice

2 tbsp (30 g) butter, melted

Caramel sauce (page 491), to serve

BANANA BREAD PUDDING

Bread pudding is one of my favorite desserts. I could eat it every day, cold or hot. This bread pudding is made with banana bread, and it is the best thing ever. It takes only minutes to make, which is dangerous because that means I can make this as often as I like.

Spritz six ramekins with the spray oil.

In a large bowl, whisk together the eggs, butter, milk, sugar, vanilla and cinnamon.

Add the bread cubes to the egg mixture and use a spoon to squish all of the bread into the egg mixture. Let the bread sit for about 5 minutes to absorb the liquid.

Fill each of the prepared ramekins three-quarters full of the bread pudding.

Put three to four ramekins in the air fryer and air-fry the bread pudding at 330°F (166°C) for 20 minutes. Repeat this process with the remaining ramekins.

TIP: This bread pudding is great warm, but I also love it cold from the fridge!

MAKES:
6 SERVINGS

Spray oil

3 large eggs

2 tbsp (30 ml) melted butter

1½ cups (360 ml) milk

6 tbsp (72 g) sugar

1 tsp pure vanilla extract

½ tsp cinnamon

6 slices banana bread, cubed

VANILLA–ALMOND POUND CAKE

Everyone wants to make pound cake fancy, but I believe that a good pound cake needs simple flavoring—a little vanilla and a little almond make the absolute best pound cake.

Spray six silicone or foil cupcake liners with the spray oil.

In a large bowl, use a hand mixer to beat the butter and sugar for 2 to 3 minutes, until the mixture is light and fluffy. Slowly beat in the eggs, one at a time, then add the vanilla and almond extract.

In a small bowl, whisk together the flour and baking powder.

With a wooden spoon, fold the flour mixture into the butter mixture until the batter is smooth.

Divide the batter among the prepared cupcake liners. Sprinkle the sliced almonds on top of the batter, dividing them as evenly as possible.

Air-fry three or four cupcakes at a time at 330°F (166°C) for 12 to 15 minutes, until a toothpick inserted in the center comes out clean. Remove the cupcakes from the air fryer and let them cool completely. Meanwhile, repeat this process with the remaining cupcakes.

TIP: You can switch out the almond extract for lemon extract for a citrusy spin on this cake. Some whipped cream and fresh fruit make this the perfect dessert.

MAKES: 6 CUPCAKES

Spray oil

½ cup (120 g) butter, softened

1 cup (192 g) sugar

2 large eggs

1 tsp pure vanilla extract

1 tsp pure almond extract

¾ cup (90 g) flour

½ tsp baking powder

2 tbsp (14 g) sliced almonds

COOKIES AND CREAM BUNDLES

Cookies and cream is everyone's favorite dessert flavor, right? I wrap chocolate sandwich cookies in flaky dough, then I pop the bundles into the air fryer for a few minutes to make a delectably sinful dessert. A sprinkle of powdered sugar is all you need to garnish this spectacular little treat.

Place a parchment round in the air fryer basket and spritz it with the spray oil.

Roll out the crescent roll dough and pinch the seams to make a single piece of dough.

Cut the dough into eight equal pieces. Place a chocolate sandwich cookie in the middle of each square of dough and fold the dough over completely to cover the cookie.

Place the bundles in the air fryer and air-fry them at 320°F (160°C) for 6 minutes.

Dust the bundles with the powdered sugar prior to serving.

MAKES: 8 BUNDLES

Spray oil

1 (8-oz [227-g]) can crescent rolls

8 chocolate sandwich cookies

Powdered sugar

ACKNOWLEDGMENTS

This book was a labor of love and would not have been possible without some amazing people in my life who helped:

To my husband, Daniel, who kept me going even when I was exhausted; cleaned up after I was cooking and photographing all day; and kept me stocked up with the "good ice" for the long nights of typing. Love you, babe!

For my boys, Sam and Dean, who are the reason I work hard so I can provide them with everything. They are my everything.

To my mom, Paige, who taught me how to work hard and never give up.

To my grandma, Milinda, who spent her afternoons in school pickup lines and entertaining my boys so I could get work done.

To the rest of my family, for being such an amazing support system and my biggest cheerleaders.

To my blog readers, I could not be where I am today, realizing my dream of writing cookbooks, without you.

To my editor, Marissa Giambelluca, for making this such an easy and exhilarating process and for helping me create a book I am so proud of.

To Page Street Publishing for being a fabulous company that I am so excited to be working with! Their cookbooks are gorgeous—I love them, and I am so happy to be working with Page Street.

And to all of you who have purchased this book, thank you so much for supporting me and my book.

ABOUT THE AUTHOR

Parrish Ritchie is a nap-deprived, taco-obsessed, married mom of two rambunctious boys living in Virginia. When she's not wrangling kids, making dinners or bingeing Netflix, she blogs at LifeWithTheCrustCutOff.com, serving up recipes anyone can make and everyone will love. She has been blogging for more than ten years and has been featured on Food Network, *Redbook, Woman's Day*, the *TODAY* show, HuffPost, BuzzFeed, Family Fun and more.

INDEX